Irish Place Names

P. W. Joyce

First published in 1984 by

The Appletree Press Ltd
The Old Potato Station
14 Howard Street South
Belfast BT7 1AP

Tel: +44 (028) 90 24 30 74
Fax: +44 (028) 90 24 67 56
Email: reception@appletree.ie
Web: www.appletree.ie

Copyright © Appletree Press, 1984, 2006
Photographs © John Murphy, 2006
Additional Photographs © As acknowledged on page 128

A catalogue record for this book is available from the British Library.

Irish Place Names

ISBN-13: 978 0 86281 993 4
ISBN-10: 0 86281 993 8

Desk and Marketing Editor: Jean Brown
Editor: Jim Black
Designer: Stuart Wilkinson
Production Manager: Paul McAvoy

9 8 7 6 5 4 3 2 1

AP3266

Contents

A Note from the Publisher

The author, Patrick Weston Joyce, was born in Glenosheen, County Limerick, in 1827. A teacher by profession, he published a number of collections of Irish songs, several histories of Ireland and a collection of Gaelic folk tales, as well as the popular work *English as we Speak it in Ireland* (1910), a study of dialect variations. Perhaps his best known work, however, is *The Origin and History of Irish Names of Places* (three volumes). He died in Dublin in 1914.

This book was originally published in 1870 under the title *Irish Local Names Explained*.

Note: For ease of use we refer to Offaly and Laois rather than the titles given in the original (King's County and Queen's County respectively). King's County was renamed Offaly in 1920 and Queen's County was renamed Laois in 1922.

Introduction

The Process of Anglicising

1.   Systematic Changes

Irish pronunciation preserved: In anglicising Irish names, the leading general rule is that the present forms are derived from the ancient Irish as they were spoken, not as they were written. Those who first committed them to writing aimed at preserving the original pronunciation by representing it as nearly as they were able in English letters.

Generally speaking, this principle explains the alterations that were made in the spelling of names in the process of reducing them from ancient to modern forms. Allowing for the difficulty of representing Irish words by English letters, it will be found that, on the whole, the ancient pronunciation is fairly preserved.

Aspiration: The most common causes of change in the reduction of Irish names are aspiration and eclipsis. Some of the Irish consonants are in certain situations subject to what is called aspiration; it is indicated by the letter *h*, and it always changes the sound of the consonants.

B and *m* aspirated (*bh, mh*) are both sounded like *v* or *w* in the English form: examples, Ardvally in Donegal and Sligo, in Irish *Ardbhaile*, high town; Ballinwully in Roscommon, *Baile-an-mhullaigh*, the town of the summit (*mullach*). Sometimes they are represented by *t* in English as in Boherduff, *Bothar-dubh*, black road, and often they are suppressed especially in the end of words or between two vowels as in Knockdoo, *Cnoc-dubh*, black hill, the same as Knockduff in other places.

For *c* aspirated, see p. 9.

D and *g* aspirated (*dh, gh*), have a faint guttural sound not existing in English and they are consequently generally unrepresented in anglicised names as in Lisnalee, *Lios-na-laegh*, the fort of the calves.

7

F aspirated (*fh*) totally loses its sound in Irish and of course is omitted in English as in Knockanree in Wicklow, *Cnoc-an-fhraeigh*, the hill of the heath.

P aspirated is represented by *f*, as in Ballinfoyle, *Baile-an-phoill*, the town of the hole the same as *Ballinphuill* and *Ballinphull* elsewhere.

S and *t* aspirated (*sh*, *th*) both sound the same as English *h*, as in Drumhillagh in Cavan and Monaghan, *Druim-shaileach*, the ridge of the sallows, the same name as Drumsillagh in other counties in which the original *s* sound is retained.

Eclipsis: An eclipsed consonant has its sound altogether suppressed, the sound of another consonant which is prefixed being heard instead. Thus when *d* is eclipsed by *n*, it is written *n-d*, but the *n* alone is pronounced. The eclipsed letter is of course always omitted in English.

When a noun is used in the genitive plural, with the article prefixed, its initial consonant is eclipsed. Each consonant has a special eclipsing letter of its own.

B is eclipsed by *m*. Knocknamoe, the name of a place in Laois, represents the Irish *Cnoc-na-mbo*, the hill of the cows.

C is eclipsed by *g*, as in Cloonnagashel near Ballinrobe which ought to have been anglicised Coolnagashel, for the Four Masters write the name *Cuil-na-gcaiseal*, the corner of the cashels or stone forts.

D and *g* are both eclipsed by *n*, as in Mullananallog in Monaghan, *Mullach-na-ndealg*, the summit of the thorns or thorn bushes.

F is eclipsed by *bh* which is represented by *v* in English as in Carrignavar in Cork which is in Irish *Carraig-na-bhfear*, the rock of the men.

P is eclipsed by *b*, as in Gortnaboul in Kerry and Clare, *Gort-na-bpoll*, the field of the holes.

S is eclipsed by *t* in the genitive singular with the article as in Ballintaggart, *Baile-an-tsagairt*, the town of the priest.

T is eclipsed by *d* as in Lisnadurk in Fermanagh *Lios-na-dtorc*, the fort of the boars.

2.   Corruptions

While the majority of names have been modernised in accordance with the principle of preserving the pronunciation, great numbers on the other hand have been contracted and corrupted in a variety of ways. Some of these corruptions took place in the Irish language but far the greatest number were introduced by the English-speaking people in transferring the words from the Irish to the English language. The following are some of the principal corruptions.

Interchange of l, m, n, r. The interchange of these letters is common in Irish and English as well as in other languages. We find *l* very often substituted for *r*, as in Shrule, Shruel, Struell, Sroohill, in all of which the final consonant sound should be that of *r*, for they are derived from *Sruthair* (sruher), as stream.

N is sometimes but not often changed to *l*, as in Castleconnell near Limerick which is the castle of the O'Connings, not of the O'Connells as the present form of the name would indicate.

The change of *n* to *r* is of frequent occurrence, as in Kilmacrenan in Donegal, which should have been called Kilmacnenn for the Irish authorities write it *Cill-mac-nEnain*, which Colgan translates the church of the sons of Enan who were contemporaries and relatives of St Columba.

The change of *l* to *r* is not very common but we find it in Ballysakeery in Mayo which is written by Mac-Firbis *Baile-easa-caoile* (Ballysakooly), the town of the narrow cataract.

M and *n* are occasionally interchanged. For example, the barony of Glenquin in Limerick should have been called Glenquim for the Irish is *Gleann-a'-chuim*, the glen of the *cum* or hollow. Kilmainham near Dublin is called Kilmannan by Boate which is more correct than the present form. The name signifies the church of St Mainen (Irish *Maighnenn*), who was bishop and abbot there in the seventh century.

Change of ch *and* th *to* f. The guttural sound of *c* aspirated (*ch*) does not exist in English, and in anglicised names it is occasionally changed to *f*, for example, Knocktopher in Kilkenny is from the Irish *Cnoc-a'-tochair*, the hill of the *togher* or causeway. *F* is also sometimes

9

substituted for *th*: thus Tiscoffin in Kilkenny took its name from an old church called *Tigh-scoithin* (Tee-Scoheen), the house of St Scoithin who erected his primitive church here towards the close of the sixth century.

Substitution of g *for* d. *D* aspirated is often changed to *g*, as in Drumgonnelly in Louth which should have been anglicised Drumdonnelly for the Irish is *Druim-Dhonghaile*, the ridge or long hill of the Donnellys.

Addition of d *after* n, *and of* b *after* m. The letter *d* is often corruptly placed after *n* as we find in the case of Rathfriland in Down which is called in Irish *Rath-Fraeileann*, Freelan's fort. *B* is also often placed after *m*, as in Cumber or Comber, the names of several places in the northern counties. The Irish word is *Comar* which signifies the confluence of two waters and is correctly anglicised Cummer and Comer in many other names.

Note

The following abbreviations have been used in quoting authorities for the Irish forms:

'F.M.,' *The Annals of the Four Masters*.
'Book of R.,' *The Book of Rights* (*Leabhar-na-gCeart*).
'Hy F.,' *The Tribes and Customs of Hy Fiachrach*.
'O'Dugan,' The topographical Poems of O'Dugan and O'Heeren.
'O'C. Cal.,' O'Clery's Calendar of Irish Saints, or, *The Martyrology of Donegal*.
'Wars of GG.,' *The Wars of the Gaedhill with the Gaill* (of the Irish with the Danes).
'Mart. Tam.,' *The Martyrology of Tallaght*.

The Irish forms are always in italics. The Irish root words are fully explained in the following section.

The pronunciation of the principal Irish words is given in brackets as nearly as can be represented by English letters.

Irish Root Words

The principal modern forms are given in italics.

Abh (aw or ow) a river; *aw, ow.*

Abhainn (owen) a river; *owen, avon,* and in the end of words, with the h of the article, *hown, hone, howna, hivnia.*

Abhall (owl, ool or avel) an apple, an apple tree; in some parts of the north it is used in the sense of 'orchard'. Modern forms owl, ool, awle, aval, etc.

Achadh (aha) a field; it is generally represented in modern names by *agha, agh* or *augh* but these also often stand for *ath,* a ford.

Aenach (enagh) anciently signified any assembly of the people but it is now always applied to a cattle fair; *engah, eeny, eena, eanig.*

Aileach (ellagh) a circular stone fort; *ellagh, elly.*

Aill (oil) a cliff; *ayle, aille,* etc. See Faill.

Aireagal (arrigal) a habitation, an oratory, a small church; *arrigle* and *errigal.*

Airne (arney) a sloe; *arneg.*

Ait (aut) a place, a site; commonly made at: frequently combines with *leach,* a house, to form the compound *ait-tighe* (aut-tee) in modern forms *atty* or *attl,* a house site.

Aiteann (attan) furze, forms the terminations *-attin, -attina.*

Aith (ah) a kiln of any kind; made *-haia, -hagh, -haha, -hay, -hey* and *-hoy* in the end of names.

Alt a height, a cliff, a glen side.

An the Irish definite article.

Ar (awr) slaughter; *aro, aur* and *air.*

Ard high, a height.

Ath (ah) a ford; *ath, ah, augh, agh, a, aha, aw,* etc.

Bád (baud) a boat.

Badhun (bawn) a cow fortress, the *bawn* of a castle.

Baile (bally) a town, a townland; *bally, balli, vally* and in the eastern counties *bal.*

Bán (bawn) white or fair coloured; *bane, baun, bawn, vane, vaun.*

Barr (baur) the top, the highest point; *bar, baur.* The Bar of a townland (used in the north) is the high or hilly part.

Beag (beg) little.

Bealach (ballagh) a road or pass; *ballagh*, *vally*.

Bealtaine (beltany) the first day of May; celebrated as a festival by the pagan Irish.

Beann (ban, ben) a horn, a gable, a peak or pointed hill.

Beannchar (banaher) horns, gables, peaks; *banagher*, *bangor*.

Bearn, **bearna**, **bearnas** (barn, barna, barnas) a gap, a gap in a mountain; *barna*, *barny*, *varna*, *varny*, *barnis*, *varnis*, and often in the north *barnet*.

Bearnach (barnagh) gapped.

Beith (beh) the birch tree; *beitheach* (behagh) a birchy place; *behy*, *beha*, *beagh*, *behagh*, *veha*, *vehy*, etc.

Bél, **beul** (bale) the mouth, an entrance, a ford; often joined to ath in the compound *bél-atha* (bellaha, bella), a ford-mouth or ford entrance.

Bile (billa) a large ancient tree; a tree held in veneration for any reason; *billa*, *billy*, *villa*, *ville*, *villy*, *bella*, *vella*.

Biorar (birrer) watercress; usually corrupted to *biolar* (biller); *viller*, *vilra*, etc.

Bo a cow; *bo*, *boe*, and by eclipse, *moe* (mbo); see page 8.

Boireann (burren) a large rock, a rocky district.

Both (boh) a tent or hut; *bo*, *boh*, *boha*, *bohy*, *voe*.

Bóthar (boher) a road; *boher* and *voher*. In some of the eastern counties it is corrupted to batter. Bohereen, a little road.

Braghad (braud) the throat; a gorge; *braid*, *broad*, *braud*.

Bran a raven.

Breach (breagh) a wolf; occurs in the compound *breach-mhagh* (breaghvah), wolf-field.

Bri (bree) a hill; *bree*, *bray*.

Broc (bruck) a badger; *brock*, *brick* and by eclipse *mrock*; see page 8.

Brocach (bruckagh) a badger warren; *brockagh*, *brocky*.

Brugh (bru) a palace, a distinguished residence; *bru*, *bruff*. Bruighean (breean) has the same meaning but in modern times it is used to denote a fairy palace; *breen*, *bryan*, *breena*, *vreena*.

Buaile (boolia) a booley, a feeding or milking place for cows; *booley*, *boley*, *boola*, *voola*, *voula*, *vooly*.

Buidhe (bwee or boy) yellow; *boy*, *wee*, etc.

Buirghes (burris) a burgage or borough; *borris* and *burris*.

Bun the end or bottom of anything; the mouth of a river.

Cabhan (cavan) a hollow; in some parts of Ulster it signifies a round hill; *cavan*.

Caech (kay) blind, purblind, one-eyed; *keagh, kee*.

Caenach (keenagh) moss; *keenagh*.

Caera (kaira) a sheep; *keeragh* and, eclipsed with the article, *nageeragh*.

Caerthainn (kairhan) the quicken tree; *keeran, caran, kerane, keraun*.

Cairthe (carha) a pillar stone; *carra, carha* and *car*.

Caiseal (cashel) a circular stone fort; *cashel, castle*.

Caisleán (cushlaun) a castle; *cashlaun, cashlane*.

Cala a marshy meadow along a river or lake; a landing place for boats; *callow* and *cala*.

Capall a horse; *capple, cappul* and eclipsed with the article (see page 8) *nagappul* and *nagapple*.

Carn a monumental heap of stones; *carn, carna*.

Carr a rock, rocky land.

Carraig (corrig) a rock; *carrig, carrick, carriga*.

Cartron a quarter of land (Anglo-Norman).

Casan (cassaun) a path.

Cath (cah) a battle.

Cathair (caher) a circular stone fort, a city; *caher, cahir*.

Ceallurach (calluragh) an old burial ground; *calloorugh*.

Cealtrach (caltragh) an old burial ground; *caltragh, caldragh*.

Ceann (can) the head, front or highest part of anything; *kan, can, kin, ken*.

Ceapach (cappa) a plot of ground laid down in tillage; *cappagh, cappa, cap, cappy*.

Ceard (card) an artificer; *nagard, nagarde* 'of the artificers'.

Ceardcha (cardha) a forge; *carte, cart, cartan, carton*.

Ceathramhadh (carhoo) a quarter, a quarter of land; *carrow, carhoo, carrive*.

Ceide (keady) a hillock, a hill level and smooth at top; *keady, keadew, keadagh, cady, caddagh*.

Ceis (kesh) a wicker basket, a wickerwork causeway; *kish, kesh*.

Cill (kill) a church; *kill, kil, kyle, keel, cal, kille, killa*.

Cinel (kinel) kindred, race, descendants; *kinel, kinal*.

Cladh (ely or claw) a ditch; *cly, claw, cla*.

Clann children, a tribe; *clan, clan*.

Clar a board, a plain; *clar, clare*.

Clais (clash) a trench; *clash*.

Cliath (clee) a hurdle.

Cloch a stone, a stone castle; *clogh, clough, clo, clohy, cloy, naglogh.*

Clochan a row of stepping stones across a river, sometimes a stone castle; *cloghan, cloghane, cloghaun.*

Cluain (cloon) a meadow, a fertile piece of land among bogs, marshes, or woods; *cloon, clon, clin, colony.*

Cnap (knap) a knob, a round little hill; *knap, nap, crap, crup.*

Cnoc (knock) a hill; *knock, knick, nick, crock, cruck.*

Cobhlach (cowlagh) a fleet; *cowly, howly, coltig, holt.*

Coigeadh (coga) a fifth part, a province; *cooga, coogue.*

Coill a wood; *kil, kyle, cuill, cullia.*

Coinieer (knickere) a rabbit warren; *coneykeare, conecar, conigar, conigare, kinnegar, nicker,* etc.

Coínín (cunneen) a rabbit; *coneen, nagoneen, nagoneeny.*

Coll the hazel; *coll, col, cole, cull, cul, coyle, kyle, quill.*

Congbhail (congwal) a habitation, a church; *conwal, Connell, cunnagavale.*

Cor a round hill, etc.

Cora a weir; *cor, corra, curra, cur.*

Corc, corca race, progeny; *corka.*

Coreach a marsh; *corcagh, corkey, cork.*

Corr a crane or heron; *cor, gor, gore, nagor.*

Cos a foot; *cuss, cush, cosh.*

Cot a small boat; *cotty.*

Craebh (crave) a branch, a large branchy tree; *creeva, crew, creevy, nagreeve.*

Craig (crag) a rock.

Crann a tree; *crann, cran, crin, nagran.*

Crannog an artificial island or lake dwelling; *crannoge, cronoge.*

Creabhar (crour) a wood-cock; *crour, nagrour.*

Creamh (crav) wild garlic.

Croch a cross, a gallows; *crogh, crohy, crehy, creha.*

Corchaire (crohera) a hangman; *croghera, croghery, nagroghery.*

Cros a cross; *cross, crush, crusha.*

Cruach, cruachán (cruagh, cruhaun) a rick, a round stacked up hill; *crogh, cruagh, croagh, croghan, croaghan.*

Cruit (crit) a hump, a round little hill; *cruit, crotta, crutta, crit.*

Cu a fierce dog, a hound; genitive *con, con, nagon, nagun.*

Cuas (coose) a cave, a cove; *coos, coose, cose, couse, goose, gose, nagoose.*

Cuil (cooil) a corner, an angle; *cool, cole.*

Cuillionn (cullion) holly; *cullion, cullen.*

Cúm (coom) a hollow, a dell or valley enclosed, except on one side, by mountains; *coom, coum, coombe.*

Currach a marsh; *curragh, curry, curra.*

Da (daw) two; *da, daw, a.*

Daingean (dangan) a fortress; *dangan, dingin, dingle.*

Dair (dar) an oak; *dar, der, dara, darra, darraigh.*

Dairbhre (darrery) an oak forest, a place producing oaks; *darrery, dorrery, darraragh, derravara.*

Daire or **doire** (derry) an oak grove or wood; *derry, derri, der.*

Damh (dauv) an ox; *dav, dev, daw, duff, diff, aff, uff, iff,* and by eclipse, *nanav.*

Dearc, derc (derk) a cave; *derk, dirk, dark.*

Dearg (derg) red; *derg, derrig, darrig.*

Dearmhagh (darwah) oak-plain; *durrow, durra, derra.*

Disert a desert, a hermitage; *disert, desert, Dysart, dysert, ister, ester, isert, ishart, tristle.*

Domhnach (downagh) Sunday, a church; *donagh, donna, donny, don, dun.*

Draeighean (dreean) blackthorn; *dreen, drain, drin.*

Droichead (drohed) a bridge; *droghed, drehid, drought, drait.*

Druim (drum) the back, a ridge or long hill; *drum, drom, drim, dru.*

Dumha (dooa) a burial mound; *dooey, dooa, doo, doe.*

Dún (doon) a fortified fort, a kingly residence; *dun, don, doon, down.*

Dur strong.

Each (agh) a horse; *augh, agh, eigh,* etc.

Eaglais (aglish) a church; *aglish, eglish, heagles, eglir.*

Eanach (annagh) a marsh; *annagh, anna, anny.*

Eas (ass) a waterfall; *ass, ess, assy, assa.*

Eascu, eascan (asscu, asscan) an ell; *askin.*

Edar between; *eder, ader, adder.*

Eidhneán (inaun) ivy; *eidneach* (inagh) an ivy-bearing place; *inane, inagh, eany, enagh.*

Eilit (ellit) a doe; *elty, ilty, elt, ilt.*

Eisc (esk) a water channel; *esk.*

Eiscir (esker) a ridge of high land, a sand hill; *esker, iskera, ascragh, eskeragh.*

En (ain) a bird; *naneane* 'of the birds'.

Eó (o) a yew tree; *o, oe, yo.*

Eochaill (oghill) a yew wood; *oghill, aughal, youghal.*

Eudan (eden) the forehead, a hill brow; *eden, edn.*

Ey an island (Danish); *ey, i, ay, eye.*

Fada long; *fada, fad, ad, ada, adda.*

Faeileán, faeileóg (fweelaun, fweeloge) a sea gull; *naweelaun, naweeloge* ('of the sea gulls'), *wheelion, eelan.*

Faill (foyle) a cliff; *foyle, foil, fall. See* Aill.

Faithche (faha) a green level space near a residence for games, exercises, etc.; a level field; *faha, fahy, fa, foy, fy, fey, feigh.*

Fásach (faussagh) a wilderness; *fasagh, fassagh, fassa.*

Feadán (faddaun) a streamlet; *faddan, feddan, fiddan, fiddane, eddan.*

Feadóg (faddoge) a plover; *viddoge, vaddoge, faddock, feddock.*

Feannóg (fannoge) a scaldcrow; *finnoge, funnock, vannoge.*

Fear (far) a man; *fir, feara* men; *fer, fir,* and by eclipse, *navar.*

Fearann (farran) land; *farran, farn, arran.*

Fearn, fearnóg (farn, farnoge) the alder tree; *farn, fern, fernagh, ferney, farnane, farnoge, navarn, navern, navarna.*

Fearsad (farsad) a sand bank formed in a river by the opposing currents of tide and stream; *farset, farsid, farsad, fast.*

Fert, ferta a trench, a grave; *fert, farta, ferta, fartha, arta, navart.*

Fiach (feeagh) a raven; *ee, eha, eigh, naveagh.*

Fiadh (feea) a deer; *eigh, eag, nareigh.*

Fidh (fih) a wood; *fee, fi, feigh, feth, fith, fid.*

Fionn, finn (fin) white, clear, transparent; *fin, finn, fune, foun.*

Fiord a sea inlet (Danish); *ford.*

Fórnocht a bare, naked or exposed hill; *forenaght, fornaght, farnaght.*

Fraech (freagh) heath; *freagh, freugh, free, ree.*

Fuaran (fooran) a cold spring; *see* Uaran.

Fuinnse, fuinnseann, fuinnseóg (funsha, funshan, funshoge) the ash tree; *funcheon, funshin, funshinagh, funchoge.* The *f* is omitted in the north, giving rise to such forms as *unshin, unshinagh, inshinagh,* *unshog, hinchoge.*

Gabhal (goul, gole) a fork, a river fork; *goul, gole, gowel, goole, gola.*

Gabhar (gour) a goat; *gower, gour, gore.*

Gaertha (gairha) a thicket along a river; *gearha, geragh, geeragh, gairha, geary.*

Gall (Gaul) a foreigner, a Gaul; a standing stone; *gall, gal, gaul, guile, gill, gullia.*

Gallán (gallaun) a standing stone; *gallon, gullane.*

Gaeth (gwee) wind; *gee, geeha, geehy, geeth.*

Gamhan (gowan) a calf; *gowan, gown.*

Gamhnach (gownagh) a milch cow, a *stripper* (a cow not in calf but giving little milk); *gownagh, gawnagh.*

Garbh (garriv) rough, rugged; *garriff, garve, garra.*

Garrán (garraun) a shrubbery; *garran, garrane, garraun, garn.*

Gárrdha (gaura) a garden; *garra, garry.*

Gédh (gay) a goose; *gay.*

Glaise, **glais**, **glas** (glasha, glash, glas) a streamlet; *glasha, glash, glas, glush.*

Glas green; *glass.*

Gleann (glan) a glen or valley; *glen, glin, glynn, glan, glanna.*

Gniomh (gneeve) a measure of land; *gneeve.*

Gobha, gen. **gobhan** (gow, gown) a smith; *gow, goe, go, gown, gowan, guivna.*

Gorm green; *gorm.*

Gort a tilled field; *gort, gurt, gart.*

Greuch (greagh) a marshy place; *greagh, greugh.*

Graig a village; *graigue, grag, greg.*

Grian (greean) the sun; *green, gren, greany.*

Grianan (greenan) a summer house, a palace; *greenan, greenane, greenaun, grenan, grennan.*

Guala (goola) the shoulder, a hill; *goolan, golden.*

Imleach (imlagh) a marsh on the margin of a lake or river; *emlagh, emly, imilagh.*

Inbhear (inver) the mouth of a river; *inver, enner, ineer.*

Inis (inish) an island, a low meadow along a river; *inis, inish, ennis, inch.*

Iolar (iller) an eagle; *iller, uller, ilra, ulra, illard.*

Iomaire (ummera) a ridge or long hill; *ummera, ummery, umry, amery.*
Iubhar (yure) a yew tree; *ure.*

Ladhar (lyre, lear) a fork, a fork formed by glens or rivers; *lyre, lear.*
Laegh (lay) a calf; *loe, lea, leigh.*
Lag, lug a hollow, a hollow in a mountain; *lag, lig, leg, lug.*
Lágh (law) a hill; *law, la.*
Lann a house, a church; *lan, lann, land, lynn, lyn.*
Lárach (lauragh) a mare; *lara, laragh.*
Lathair, lathrach (lauher, lauragh) a site, a site of a building; *laragh, lauragh.*
Lax a salmon (Danish); *lax, leix.*
Leaba, leabaidh (labba, labby) a bed, a grave; *labba, labby.*
Leac, lic, liag (lack, lick, leeg) a flagstone; *lack, leck, lick, leek, leege.*
Leaca, Leacán (lacka, lackan) the side of a hill; *lackan lacken, lackaun, leckan, leckaun, lacka.*
Leacht (light) a monumental heap of stones; *light, lat, let, lett.*
Leamh, leamhan (lav, lavaun) the elm tree; *levan, levane, livaun, laune, lamph.*
Leamhchoill (lavwhill) an elm wood; *laughil, laghil, laghile, loghill, loughill, lamfield, longfield.*
Learg, leargaidh, leargan (larg, largy, largan) the side or slope of a hill; *largy, largan.*
Leath (lah) half; *lah, la, le.*
Leathard (lahard) half height, a gentle hill; *lahard, lard.*
Léim (lame) a leap; *leam, lem, lim.*
Leithinnsi (lehinshi) half island, a peninsula; *lehinch, lahinch, lynch.*
Leitir (letter) a wet side of a hill, plural **leatracha** (latraha); *letter, lattera, lettera, letteragh.*
Liagán (leagaun) a pillar stone; *legan, legane, legaun, leegane, leagan.*
Liath (leea) grey; *lea.*
Liathmhuine (leewinny) grey shrubbery; *leaffony, leafin, liafin, lefinn, leighmoney.*
Lios (lis) a circular earthen fort; *lis, les, lish, lass, lassa.*
Loch a lake; *lough, low.*
Loisgreán (luskraun) corn burnt in the ear; *luskraun, loskeraun, loskeran, lustraun, lustran, lustrin.*
Loisgthe (luska) burnt, burnt land; *lusky, losky, lusk.*
Lon, londubh (lon, londuv) a blackbird; *lun.*

Long a ship; *long*.
Longphort (longfort) a fortress; *longford, lonart, lunkard*.
Lurga, lurgan the shin, a long low hill; *lurraga, lurgan*.

Machaire (mahera) a plain; *maghera, maghery*.
Mac-tire (macteera) a wolf; *micteera, victeera*.
Madadh, madradh (madda, maddra) a dog; *maddy, maddoo, maddra, vaddy, vaddoo, vaddra*.
Madhm (maum) an elevated mountain pass; *maum, moym*.
Mael (mwail) bald, a hornless cow, a bald or bare hill; *moyle, meel, mweel*.
Maethail (mwayhil) soft, spongy land; *mholl, mothel, mothell, mehill, moyle, weehill*.
Magh (maw) a plain; *moy, ma, may, moigh, moig, muff, mo*.
Más (mauce) the thigh, a long low hill; *mace, mas, maas, mass*.
Meall (mall) a lump, a round little hill; *maul*.
Míliuc (meeluck) low marshy ground; land near a lake or river; *meelick, mellick*.
Min (meen) smooth, fin, small; *meen*.
Moin (money) a bog; *mone, mon, mona, vone*.
Mór (more) great, large; *more, mor*.
Móta a moat, a high mound; *moat, mota, mote*.
Mothar (moher) in the north, a cluster of trees; in the south, the ruin of a fort or of any building; *moher*.
Muc (muck) a pig; *muck, mucky*.
Muilean (mullen) a mill; *mullen, mullin, willin*.
Muine (money) a shrubbery; *money*
Muintir (munter) family, people; *munter*.
Muirisc (murrisk) a seaside marsh; *murrisk*.
Mullach (mullagh) a summit; *mullagh, mulla, mully, mul*.
Murbhach (murvah) a salt marsh along the sea; *murvagh, murvey, murragh, murreagh, murrow*.

Nás (nauce) an assembly place; *naas, nash*.
Nead (nad) a bird's nest; *nad, ned, nid, neth*.

Óg (oge) young, little; *oge, og, ock*.
Oileán (oilaun) an island; *illan, illane, illaun*.

Omna an oak; *omna, umna*.
Os a fawn; *uss, ish*.

Piast (peeast) a beast, a worm, a serpent; *piast, peastia, beast*.
Pobul (pubble) people; *pubble, pobble, popple, pobul, phubble*.
Poll a hole; *poll, poul, pull, pool, foyle, phuill, phull*.
Preachán (prehaun) a crow; *preghaun*.
Puca (pooka) a *pooka* or sprite; *pooka, puck, pook, phuca*.

Rath (raw) a circular fort; *rath, raw, rah, ray, ra, raha*.
Reidh (ray) a coarse mountain flat; *rea, re, rey*.
Reilig (rellig) a cemetery; *relick, relig*.
Riabhach (reeagh) grey; *reagh, rea*.
Riasc (reesk) a marsh; *riesk, reisk, risk, reask*.
Rince, rinceadh (rinka) dance; *rinky, rinka, rink*.
Rinn a point of land; *rin, rine, reen, ring, ranna*.
Ros generally means a wood in the south and a peninsula in the north; *ross, rus, rush*.
Rusg a marsh; *roosk, rusk, rusky*.

Saer (sair) a carpenter; *seer, teer*.
Sagart a priest; *saggart, taggart, teggart*.
Saileach (saulagh) a sallow; *sillagh, sallagh, sill*.
Samhain (sowen, savin) the first of November; *souna, sawna, hawan, haman, haven, hawna*.
Scairbh (scarriff) a shallow rugged ford; *skarriff, scarry, scarva, scarvy, scarragh*.
Scairt (scart) a thicket; *scart, scarty*.
Sceach (skagh) a whitethorn bush; *skeagh, skehy, skey, ske, skeha, skew*.
Scealp (skalp) a cleft; *scalp*.
Sceilig (skellig) a rock; *skellig*.
Sceir (sker) a sharp rock, plural **sceire** (skerry); *sker, skerry, skerries*.
Scrin (screen) a shrine; *screen, skryne, skreena*.
Seabhac (shouk) a hawk; *shoke, chock, touk, tuke*.
Sealán (shallan) a hangman's rope, a gallows; *shallon, shallan*.
Sealg (shallog) hunting; *shallog, shellig*.
Sean (shan) old; *shan, shanna*.

Seiseadh (shesha) a sixth part; *shesha, sheshia, sheshiv.*

Seisreach (shesheragh) a measure of land; *sheshera, shesheragh, sistra.*

Seiscenn (sheskin) a marsh, a quagmire; *sheskin, seskin, teskin.*

Sidh (shee) a fairy hill, a fairy; *shee.*

Sidheán (sheeaun) a fairy hill; *sheaun, sheehaun, sheean, shean, sion, shane.*

Siol (sheel) seed, descendants; *shil, shel.*

Sionnach (shinnagh) a fox; *shinny, shinnagh, tinny.*

Slíabh (sleeve) a mountain; *slieve, slie, sle, lieve, lie,* and by an eclipse of *s, tleva, tlieve, tlea.*

Slighe (slee) a road or pass; *slee.*

Sluagh (sloo) a host; *sloe, tloe, tloy, tlowig.*

Snamh (snauv) swimming, a swimming ford; *snauv, snave, sna, tna, tra.*

Sradbhaile (sradvally) street-town, a town with one street; *stradbally.*

Sraid (sraud) a street; *sraud, straid, strade, strad.*

Srón (srone) the nose, a nose-like hill; *sroad, shrone, stran.*

Sruth (sruh) a stream; *sruh, srue, srough, strew.*

Sruthair (sruher) a stream; *shrule, shruel, struell, srool, sroohill.*

Sruhán (sruhaun) a stream; *sroughan, sruffaun, straffan, truan, trone.*

Ster a place (Danish).

Stuaic (stook) a pointed pinnacle, an out-jutting point of rock; *stook.*

Suidhe (see) a sitting place, a seat; *see, se, sea, shi.*

Taebh (tave) the side, a hillside; *teeve, teev.*

Taimhleacht (tavlaght) a plague-grave, a place where those who died of a plague were interred; *tallaght, tamlaght, tamlat, tawlaqt, towlaght, toulett, howlaght, hawlagh, hamlat, hamlet.*

Tamhnach (tawnagh) a green field; *tawnagh, tawny, tonagh, tamnagh, tamny.*

Tarbh (tarriv) a bull; *tarriv, terriff, tariff, tarf, tarry, herriff, harriff.*

Tate, tath a measure of land; *tat, tate.*

Teach (tagh) a house; *tagh, ta, tee, ti, ty;* and by corruption, *sta, sti, sty.*

Teamhair (tawer) an elevated spot commanding an extensive view; *tara, touragh, tower, taur.*

Teampull (tampul) a church; *temple.*

Teine (tinna) fire; *tinny, tenny.*

Teotán (totaun) a burning or conflagration; *totaun.*

Tobar, **tipra** (gen. **tioprad**) a well; *tober*, *tubber*, *tipper*, *tubbrid*, *tibret*.
Tóchar (togher) a causeway over a bog or marsh; *togher*.
Tor a tower, a tower-like rock; *tor*.
Torc (turk) a boar; *turk*, *torc*, *hirk*, *nadurk*.
Traigh (tra) a strand; *tra*, *traw*, *tray*.
Trian (treen) a third part; *treen*, *trean*, *trien*.
Triucha (truha) a cantred or district; *trough*, *true*.
Tromm the elder or boor-tree; *trim*, *trom*, *trum*.
Tuaim (toom) a tumulus or burial mound; *toome*, *tom*, *toom*, *tum*.
Tuar (toor) a bleach green, any green field where things were put to
    bleach or dry; *toor*, *tore*, *tour*.
Tulach (tulla) a little hill; *tulla*, *tullow*, *tullagh*, *tully*, *tul*.
Turlach (toorlagh) a lake that dries up in summer; *turlough*, *turly*.

Ua a grandson, a descendant; plural **ui** or **uibh** (ee, iv) descendants;
    O (in such names as O'Brien), *hy*, *i*, *ive*.
Uagh, **uaimh** (ooa, ooiv) a cave, gen. **uamhann** (ooan); forms the
    terminations *oe*, *oo*, *nahoe*, *nahoo*, *oova*, *ove*, *one*, *oon*.
Uaran (ooran) a cold spring; *oran*.
Ubhall (ool) an apple; *see* abhall.
Uisce (iska) water; *iska*, *isky*, *isk*.
Urchur (urker) a cast or throw; *urcher*.
Urnaidhe (urny) a prayer, a prayer-house or oratory, *urney*, and with the
    article incorporated, *nurny*.

Guide to Irish Place Names

St Patrick's Cathedral on the hills of Armagh, Co. Armagh

Abbeyfeale, in Limerick: *Mainister-na-Feile*, the monastery or abbey of the river Feale.

Abbeygormican, in Galway; the abbey of the O'Cormacans.

Abbeylara (also Lara), in Longford: *Leath-rath*, F.M. (Lah-rah), half rath or fort.

Abbeyleix, the abbey of the old principality of Leix, so-called from a monastery founded there in 1183 by Conor O'Moore. In the reign of Felimy the Law-giver (AD111 to 119), this territory was given by the king of Leinster to *Lughaidh Laeighseach* (Lewy Leeshagh), Conall Carnach's grandson, for helping to expel the Munstermen who had seized on Ossory. Lewy's descendants, the O'Moores, took from him the tribe name, *Laeighis* (Leesh), and their territory was called by the same name, now modernised to Leix.

Abbeyshrule, in Longford; from a monastery founded there by one of the O'Farrells. It was anciently called *Sruthair* (Sruher), F.M., i.e. the stream of which Shrule is a corruption.

Abbeystrowry, in Cork; the same name as above. The *sruthair* or stream from which it was called, gave name also to Bealnashrura (the *beal* or ford-mouth of the stream) a village situated at an ancient ford.

Achonry, in Sligo; *Achadh-Chonaire* (Aha-Conary), F.M., Conary's field.

Adare, in Limerick; *Ath-dara* (Ahdara), F.M., the ford of the oak tree. A large oak must have anciently overshadowed the old ford on the Maigue.

Addergoole (also Addragool, Adrigole, Adrigoole), *Eadar-dha-ghabhal* (Adragoul), i.e. (a place) between two (river) forks.

Aderrig, *Ath-dearg*, red ford. *See* Aghaderg.

Affane, on the Blackwater below Cappoquin: *Atha-mheadhon* (Ah-vane), F.M., middle ford.

Agha, in several counties: *Achadh* (Aha), a field.

Aghaboe, in Laois, where St Canice of Kilkenny had his principal church. Adamnan in his Life of St Columkille, written in the seventh century, has the following passage which settles the meaning: 'St Canice being in the monastery which is called in Latin *Campulus bovis* (i.e. the field of the cow), but in Irish *Ached-bou*.'

Aghaboy, *Achadh-buidhe* (Aha-boy), yellow field.

Aghacross, near Kildorrery in Cork: the ford of the cross; probably from a cross erected in connexion with St Molaga's adjacent establishment, to mark a ford on the Funcheon. *See* Templemolaga.

Aghada, near Cork: *Ath-fhada* (Ahada), long ford.

Aghaderg, *Ath-dearg*, red ford. *See* Aderrig.

Aghadoe, near Killarney: *Achadh-dá-eó* (Aha-daw-o), F.M., the field of the two yew trees.

Aghadowey, in Derry: *Achadh-Dubhthaigh* (Ahaduffy), O'C. Cal., Duffy's field.

Achadown (also Aghadoon), the field of the *dun* or fort.

Aghadreen (also Aghadreenagh, Aghadreenan, Aghadrinagh), the field of the *dreens* or sloe bushes (*draeighean*).

Aghafad (also Aghafadda), long field.

Aghagallon, the field of the *gallan* or standing stone.

Aghagower, in Mayo: the correct name would be Aghafower, for the ancient form, as found in the old Lives of St Patrick, is *Achadh-fobhair*, the field of the spring, from a celebrated well now called St Patrick's well. The present form is written in Hy F. *Achadh-gabhair* which means the field of the goat.

Aghamore, *Achadh-mór*, great field.

Aghanloo, *Athan-Lugha*, Lugh's or Lewy's little ford.

Aghavea, in Fermanagh: *Achaah-beithe* (Ahabehy), F.M., the field of the birch trees.

Achaveagh, in Donegal and Tyrone; same as last.

Aghavilla (also **Aghaville**, **Aghavilly**), *Achadh-bhile*, the field of the *bile* or old tree.

Aghaviller, in Kilkenny: *Achadh-biorair* (Ahabirrer), F.M., the field of the watercresses (*r* changed to *l*).

Aghindarragh, in Tyrone: the field of the oak.

Aghintamy, near Monaghan: *Achadh-an-tsamhaidh*, the field of the sorrel.

Aghmacart, in Laois: the field of Art's son.

Aghnamullen, in Monaghan: the field of the mills.

Aghnaskea (also **Aghnaskeagh**, **Aghnaskew**), *Achadh-na-sceach*, the field of the whitethorn bushes.

Aghowle, in Wicklow: *Achadh-abhla*, the field of the apple trees.

Aglish, *Eaglais* (aglish), a church.

Aglisheloghane, in Tipperary: the church of the *clogh-aun* or row of steeping stones.

Aglishcormick, in Limerick: St Cormac's church.

Aglishdrinagh, in Cork: *Eaglais-draeighneach*, the church of the *dreens* or sloe bushes.

Agolagh, in Antrim: *Ath-gobhlach*, forked ford.

Ahane (also Ahaun), *Athán*, little ford.

Ahaphuca, the ford of the *pooka* or sprite.

Ahascragh, in Galway; *Ath-eascrach*, F.M., the ford of the *esker* or sand-hill.

Aille, *Aill*, a cliff.

Allen, *Aillín*, a little cliff.

Alt, *Alt*, a height, the side of a glen.

Altan, little cliff or glen side.

Altaturk, the glen side of the boar (*torc*).

Altavilla, the glen side of the *bile* or old tree.

Altinure, *Alt-an-iubhair* (yure), the glen side of the yew tree.

Altnaveagh (also **Altnaveigh**), *Alt-na-bhfiach*, the cliff or glen side of the *fiachs* or ravens.

Anna, *see* Annagh.

Annabella, near Mallow; *Eanach-bile*, the marsh of the *bile* or old tree.

Annaclone, the marsh of the meadow (*cluain*).

Annacotty, near Limerick: *Ath-na-coite*, the ford of the *cot* or little boat.

Annacramph, in Armagh and Monaghan: *Eanach-creamha*, the marsh of the wild garlic.

Annaduff, *Eanach-dubh*, F.M., black marsh.

Annagh, *Fanach*, a marsh.

Annaghaskin, in Dublin, near Bray: *Eanach-easgann*, the marsh of the eels.

Annaghbeg (also **Annaghmore**), little marsh, great marsh.

Annahagh (also **Annahaia**), in Monaghan and Armagh: *Ath-na-haithe*, the ford of the kiln (*aith*).

Annahavil, *Eanach-abhaill*, the marsh of the orchard (*abhall*).

Annahilt in Down: *Eanach-eilte*, the marsh of the doe (*eilit*).

Annakisha, the ford of the *kish* or wickerwork causeway.

Annalong, in Down: *Ath-na-long*, the ford of the ships (*long*). The ford was near the place where vessels used to be moored or anchored.

Annamoe, in Wicklow: *Ath-na-mbo*, the ford of the cows (*bo*).

Anny, *see* **Annagh**.

Ardboe, in Tyrone: *Ard-bo*, the cow's height.

Ard, high, a height.

Ardagh, *Ard-achadh* (Ard-aha), high field.

Ardaghy, *see* **Ardagh**.

Ardan (also **Ardane**, **Ardaun**), little *ard* or height.

Ardara, in Donegal: *Ard-a'-raith*, the height of the rath, from a hill near the village, on which stands a conspicuous fort.

Ardataggle (also **Ardateggle**), *Ard-a'-tseagail*, the height of the rye (*seagal*).

Arbane (also **Ardbaun**), white height.

Ardbeg, little height.

Ardbraccan, in Meath: St Brecan's height. St Brecan erected a church here in the sixth century, some time previous to his removal to the great island of Aran, where he had his chief establishment.

Ardcarn, the height of the *carn* or monumental heap.

Ardcath, the height of the battle (*cath*).

Ardee, in Louth: Old English form Atherdee which represents the Irish *Ath-Fhirdia* (Ahirdee) as it is written in Irish authorities, the ford of Ferdia, a chieftain who was slain there in battle by Cuchullin in the first century.

Ardeen, in Cork and Kerry: little height.

Ardeevin, *Ard-aeibhinn*, beautiful height.

Arderin, the height of Erin or Ireland.

Ardfert, in Kerry; *Ard-ferta*, F.M., the height of the grave. Sometimes called Ardfert-Brendan, from St Brendan the navigator who founded a monastery there in the sixth century.

Ardfinnan, in Tipperary: the height of St Finan who founded a monastery there in the seventh century.

Ardgeeha, *Ard-gaeithe*, height of the wind.

Ardglass, *Ard-glas*, green height.

Ardgoul, *Ard-gabhal*, high fork.

Ardkeen, *Ardcaein*, beautiful height.

Ardkill, high church or wood (*cill* or *coill*).

Ardlougher, *Ard-luachra*, rushy height.

Ardmayle, *Ard-Maille*, F.M., Malley's height.

Ardmulchan, in Meath; *Ard-Maelchon*, F.M., Maelchon's height.

Ardnacrusha (also Ardnacrushy), the height of the cross.

Ardnageeha (also Ardnageehy), the height of the wind (*gaeth*).

Ardnamean, the height of the birds (*en*).

Ardnapreaghaun, the height of the *prehauns* or crows.

Ardnarea, near Ballina: *Ard-na-riaghadh* (reea), Hy F., the hill of the executions. Four persons were executed here in the seventh century for the murder of Kellach, bishop of Kilmore-Moy.

Ardnurcher, in Westmeath: a corruption of Athnurcher, from *Ath-an-urchair*, F.M., the ford of the cast or throw. According to a very ancient legend, a battle was fought here in the first century between the Connaught and Ulster forces. Keth Mac Magach, a Connaught chief, threw a hard round ball at Conor mac Nessa, king of Ulster, and struck him on the head from the effects of which the king died seven years afterwards.

Ardpatrick, St Patrick's height.

Ardrahan, *Ard-rathain*, the height of the ferns.

Ardskeagh, the height of the *skeaghs* or bushes.

Ardstraw, in Tyrone: *Ard-sratha* (Ard-srawha), F.M., the height of (or near) the river holm.

Ardvally, in Donegal and Sligo. *See* page 7.

Ardvarna (also **Ardvarness**, **Ardvarney**, **Ardvarnish**), *Ard-bhearna* and *Ard-bhearnas*, high gap.

Arless, in Laois: *Ard-lios*, high fort.

Armagh, written in all Irish authorities *Ard-Macha*, which, in the Book of Armagh, is translated *Altitudo Machæ*, Macha's height. From Queen Macha of the golden hair, who founded the palace of Emania, 300 years BC.

Armoy, in Antrim: *Airthir-Maighe* (Arhir-moy, F.M.), eastern plain.

Artimacormack, in Antrim: *Ard-tighe-Mic-Cormaic*, the height of Mac Cormack's house.

Artrea, in Derry: *Ard-Trea* (Mart. Taml.), Trea's height. The virgin St Trea flourished in the fifth century.

Askeaton took its name from the cataract on the Deel near the town which the F.M. call *Eas-Gephtine* (Ass-Geftine), Gephtine's cataract.

Assan (also Assaun), small *ass* or waterfall.

Assaroe, at Ballyshannon. The Book of Leinster states that *Aedh-Ruadh* (Ay-roo), queen Macha's father (*see* Armagh), was drowned in this cataract which was thence called from him *Eas-Aedha-Ruaidh* (Assayroo), *Aedh-Ruadh's* waterfall.

Assey, on the Boyne in Meath. The F.M. record that in AD524 'the battle of *Ath-Sithe* (Ah-Shee) was gained by *Muircheartach* (king of Ireland) against the Leinstermen where *Sithe* (Shee) the son of *Dian* was slain, from whom *Ath-Sithe* (*Sithe's* ford) is called.'

Athenry, *Ath-na-riogh* (ree), F.M., the ford of the kings.

Athgoe, in Dublin: the ford of the *gow* or smith.

Athlacca, in Limerick: from a ford on the Morning Star river, called *Ath-leacach*, stony ford.

Athleague, in Roscommon: *Ath-liag*, F.M., the ford of stones.

Athlone, from the ancient ford over the Shannon called in Irish authorities *Ath-Luain*, the ford of *Luan*, a man's name.

Athneasy, in Limerick: called in the F.M., *Ath-na-nDiese* (Athnaneasy), the ford of (the tribe of) the *Desii*, who inhabited the old territory of *Deisbeag*, round Knockany.

Athnid, in Tipperary: the ford of the *nead* or bird's nest.

Athnowen, a parish near Ballincollig in Cork: from a ford on the river Bride, called *Ath-'n-umahainn* (Athnooan), the ford of the cave (*uaimh*), from the great limestone cave at 'The Ovens' near the ford.

Athy, One of the battles between Lewy and the Munstermen (*see* **Abbeyleix**) was fought at a ford on the Barrow where a Munster chief, *Ae*, was slain; and from him the place was called *Ath-I* (Wars of GG), the ford of *Ae*.

Attavally, *Ait-a'-bhaile*, the site of the *bally* or town.

Atti or **Atty** in the beginning of a name is the anglicised form of *áit-tighe* (aut-tee), the place or site of a house (*ait* and *teach*).

Attidermot, the site of Dermot's house.

Attiduff, the site of the black house.

Attykit, the site of *Ceat's* or Keth's house.

Aughall, in Tipperary (also **Aughil**, in Derry): *Eochaill*, the yew wood (*eo* and *coill*). *See* Youghal and Oghill.

Aughinish, *Each-inis*, F.M., the island of horses.

Aughnacloy, *Achadh-na-cloiche* (Ahanacloha), the field of the stone.

Aughnahoy, *Achadh-na-haithe*, the field of the kiln (*aith*).

Aughnanure, near Oughterard, in Galway: *Achadh-na-niúbhar* (Ahananure), the field of the yew trees. One of the old yews still remains.

Aughnish, *see* **Aughinish**.

Aughrim, the name is written in Irish document, *Each-dhruim* (Agh-rim; *dh* silent), which Colgan translates *Equi-mons*, the hill, *druim*, or ridge, of the horse (*each*).

Aughris (also **Aughrus**), *Each-ros*, F.M., the peninsula of the horses.

Avalbane (also **Avalreagh**), white orchard, grey orchard (*abhall*).

Avonmore (also **Avonbeg**), great river, little river (*abhainn*).

Aubeg, *Abh-bheag*, little river.

Ayle, *see* **Aille**.

Cliffs at Ballybunion, Co. Kerry

Bailey lighthouse, at Howth, from the old *bally* or fortress of Criffan, king of Ireland in the first century, on the site of which it was built.

Balbriggan, in Dublin: *Baile-Breacain*, Brecan's town.

Baldoyle, in Dublin: *Baile-Dubhghoill*, *Dubhgall's* or Doyle's town.

Balfeddock, the town of the *feadogs* or plovers.

Balgeeth, in Meath: the town of the wind (*gaeth*).

Balla, in Mayo. In the Life of St Mochua, we are told that before the saint founded his monastery there in the seventh century, the place was called *Ros-dairbh-reach* (Ros-dar'aragh), i.e. oak grove. He enclosed the wells of his establishment with a *balla* or wall, and hence the place received the new name of Balla.

Ballagh, *Bealach*, a road or pass.

Ballaghaderreen, in Mayo: the road of the *derreen* or little oak wood.

Ballaghbehy, the road of the birch (*beith*).

Ballaghboy, yellow road (*buidhe*).

Ballaghkeen, in Wexford: beautiful road (*caein*).

Ballaghkeeran, the road of the *keerans* or quicken trees.

Ballaghmore, great road.

Ballard, *Baile-ard*, high town.

Ballee, in Down: written in the Taxation of 1306, *Baliath*, from the Irish Baile-atha, the town of the ford.

Balleen, little *bally* or town.

Ballina, the name of many places: *Bel-an-atha* (Bellanaha), the mouth of the ford.

Ballinabarny, the town of the *bearna* or gap.

Ballinaboy, in Cork, Galway and Roscommon: *Bel-an-atha-buidhe*, the mouth of the yellow ford.

Ballinaclogh, the town of the stones (*cloch*).

Ballinacor (also **Ballinacur**, **Ballinacurra**), the mouth of the long ford.

Ballinagar, *Bel-ath-na-gcarr* (Bellanagar), the ford-mouth of the cars.

Ballinahinch, the town of the *inis* or island.

Ballinakill, the town of the church or wood.

Ballinalack, in Westmeath: *Bel-atha-na-leac* (Bellanalack), the mouth of the ford of the flagstones.

Ballinalee (also **Ballinalea**), *Bel-atha-na-laegh*, the ford-mouth of the calves.

Ballinamona, *Baile-na-mona*, the town of the bog.

Ballinamore, Bel-an-atha-moir, *the mouth of the great ford*.

Ballinamought, near Cork: *Baile-na-mbocht*, the town of the poor people (*bocht*).

Ballinard, the town of the *ard* or height.

Ballinscarty, the town of the *scart* or thicket.

Ballinasloe, *Bel-atha-na-sluaigheadh* (Bellanaslooa), F.M., the ford-mouth of the hosts or gatherings.

Ballinaspick (also **Ballinaspig**), *Baile-an-easpuig*, the town of the bishop.

Ballinastraw, the town of the *srath* or river-holm.

Ballinchalla, on Lough Mask in Mayo: *Baile-an-chala*, the town of the callow or landing place.

Ballinclare, the town of the *clar* or plain.

Ballincloghan, *see* **Ballycloghan**.

Ballincollig, *Baile-an-chullaigh*, the town of the boar.

Ballincurra (also **Ballincurrig**, **Ballincurry**), *Baile-an-chur-raigh*, the town of the *curragh* or marsh.

Ballinderry, the town of the *derry* or oak wood.

Ballindrait (also **Ballindrehid**), *Baile-an-droichid*, the town of the bridge.

Ballineddan, in Wicklow: *Baile-an-fheadáin*, the town of the *feadan* or streamlet.

Ballinfoyle, in Galway and Wicklow; *see* page 8.

Ballingaddy, the town of the thief (*gadaighe*), i.e. the black thief O'Dwane.

Ballingarrane, the town of the *garran* or shrubbery.

Ballingarry, *Baile-an-gharrdha*, the town of the garden.

Ballinglanna (also **Ballinglen**), the town of the glen.

Ballingowan, the town of the smith (*gobha*).

Ballinlass (also **Ballinlassa**, **Ballinlassy**, **Ballinliss**), the town of the *lios* or fort.

Ballinlough, the town of the lake.

Ballinloughan (also **Ballinloughaun**), the town of the little lake.

Ballinlug (also **Ballinluig**), the town of the *lug* or hollow.

Ballinphuill (also **Ballinphull**), *see* page 8.

Ballinree, sometimes *Baile-an-fhraeigh*, the town of the heath (*fraech*); sometimes *Baile-an-righ*, the town of the king.

Ballinrobe, the town of the river Robe.

Ballinrostig, Roche's town.

Ballinspittle, the town of the *spital* or hospital.

Ballintaggart, *see* page 8.

Ballinteer, *Baile-an-tsaeir*, the town of the carpenter.

Ballintemple, the town of the *temple* or church.

Ballinteskin, *Baile-an-tsescenn*, the town of the morass.

Ballintlea (also **Ballintleva**, **Ballintlevy**, **Ballintlieve**), *Baile-an-tsleibhe*, the town of the mountain (*sliabh*).

Ballintober, the town of the well.

Ballintogher, the town of the *togher* or causeway.

Ballintubbert (also **Ballintubbrid**), *see* Ballintober.

Ballinure, the town of the yew tree (*iubhar*).

Ballinvally, *Baile-an-bhealaigh*, the town of the road.

Ballinvarrig (also **Ballinvarry**), Barry's town.

Ballinvella (also **Ballinvilla**), *Baile-an-bhile*, the town of the *bile* or ancient tree.

Ballinvoher, *Baile-an-bhothair*, the town of the road.

Ballinvreena, in Limerick and Tipperary: the town of the *bruighean* (breen) or fairy mansion.

Ballinwillin, *Baile-an-mhuilinn*, the town of the mill.

Ballinwully, in Roscommon: *see* page 7.

Ballytore, in Kildare, took its name from a ford on the river Greece: *Bel-atha-a'-tuair* (Bellatoor), the ford mouth of the *tuar* or bleach green.

Ballyard, high town.

Ballybaan (also **Ballybane**, **Ballybaun**), white town.

Ballybay, in Monaghan; *Bel-atha-beithe* (Bellabehy), the ford mouth of the birch.

Ballybeg, small town.

Ballyboe, i.e. 'cow-land', a measure of land.

Ballybofey, in Donegal. The correct old name is *Srath-bofey*. Some occupier named *Fiach* or Fay must have in past times kept his cows on the holm along the Finn: *Srath-bo-Fiaich*, F.M., the river holm of Fiach's cows.

Ballyboghil, in county Dublin: the town of the *bachal* or crozier; from St Patrick's crozier.

Ballyboley, the town of the *booley* or dairy place.

Ballybough, near Dublin: *Baile-bocht*, poor town. The same as **Ballybought** in other places.

Ballyboy, in Offaly: written in Irish authorities *Baile-atha-buidhe* (Ballyboy), the town of the yellow ford. The name is common in other counties and sometimes means yellow town (*Baile-buidhe*).

Ballybrack, speckled town.

Ballybrannagh, Walsh's town. The proper name Walsh is in Irish *Breathnach* (Branagh), i.e. Briton.

Ballybunnion, in Kerry: Bunnion's town.

Ballycahan (also **Ballycahane**), O'Cahan's town.

Ballycahill, Cahill's or O'Cahill's town.

Ballycastle, in Antrim: the town of the castle.

Ballycastle, in Mayo: the town of the *cashel* or circular stone fort.

Ballyclare, *see* **Ballinclare**.

Ballyclerahan, in Tipperary: O'Clerahan's town.

Ballyclogh (also **Ballyclohy**), the town of the stones.

Ballycloghan, the town of the *cloghan* or row of stepping stones across a river.

Ballyclug, in Antrim: the town of the bell (*clog*).

Ballycolla, the town of Colla, a man's name.

Ballyconnell, in Cavan. According to tradition, Conall Carnagh, one of the most renowned of the Red Branch knights of Ulster, was slain here in the first century; hence it was called *Bel-atha-Chonaill*, the mouth of the ford of Conall.

Ballycormick, Cormac's or O'Cormac's town.

Ballycullane, O'Cullane's or O'Collins's town.

Ballydehob, in Cork: *Bel-atha-da-chab*, the ford of the two *cabs* or mouths, from some local feature.

Ballyduff, black town.

Ballyea, O'Hea's or Hayes's town.

Ballyeighter, *Baile-iochtar*, lower town.

Ballyfoyle, the town of the hole (*poll*).

Ballygarran (also **Ballygarraun**), the town of the *garran* or shrubbery.

Ballyglass, green town.

Ballygowan, the town of the smith (*gobha*).

Ballyheige, in Kerry: *Baile-ui-Thadg*, the town of O'Teige.

Ballyhooly, near Mallow: took its name from an ancient ford on the Blackwater, called in the Book of Lismore *Ath-ubhla* (Ahoola), the ford of the apples. The people now call it in Irish *Baile-atha-ubhla* (which they pronounce *Blaa-hoola*), the town of the apple ford, which has been shortened to the present name.

Ballykeel, *Baile-cael*, narrow town.

Ballyknock, the town of the hill.

Ballyknockan (also **Ballyknockane**), the town of the little hill.

Ballylanders, in Limerick: Landers's town, from an English family of that name.

Ballylig, the town of the *lug* or hollow.

Ballylongford, in Kerry: *Bel-atha-longphuirt*, the ford mouth of the *longphort* or fortress because it led to Carrigafoyle castle, two miles off.

Ballylough (also **Ballyloughan**, **Ballyloughaun**), the town of the lake.

Ballylusk (also **Ballylusky**), *Baile-loisgthe*, burnt town, from the practice of burning the surface in tillage.

Ballymena (also **Ballymenagh**), *Baile-meadhonach*, middle town.

Ballymoney, the town of the shrubbery (*muine*).

Ballymore, great town. Sometimes when the place is on a river it is *Bel-atha-moir* (Bellamore), the mouth of the great ford.

Ballymote, *Baile-an-mhota*, F.M., the town of the moat or mound.

Ballynabarna (also **Ballynabarny**, **Ballynabearne**), the town of the gap. *See* Ballinabarny.

Ballynaboley (also **Ballynaboola**, **Ballynabearna**), the town of the *booley* or dairy place (*buaile*). *See* Ballyboley.

Ballynacally, the town of the *calliagh* or hag.

Ballynacarrick (also **Ballynacarrig**, **Ballynacarriga**, **Ballynacarrigy**), the town of the rock (*carraigh*).

Ballynaclogh (also **Ballynacloghy**), *Baile-na-cloiche*, the town of the *cloch* or stone.

Ballynacor (also **Ballynacorra**), the town of the weir (*cora*).

Ballynacourty, the town of the *court* or mansion.

Ballynagall (also **Ballynagaul**), the town of the *Galls* or foreigners.

Ballynagard, the town of the *ceards* or artificers.

Ballynagee (also **Ballynageeha**), town of the wind (*gaeth*).

Ballynageeragh, the town of the sheep (*caera*).

Ballynaglogh, *Baile-nagcloch*, the town of the stones.

Ballynagore, the town of the goats (*gabhar*).

Ballynagowan, the town of the smiths (*gobha*).

Ballynagran, *Baile-na-gcrann*, the town of the trees.

Ballynahaglish, the town of the church (*eaglais*).

Ballynahinch, the town of the *inish* or island.

Ballynahone (also **Ballynahown**, **Ballynahowna**), the town of the river (*abhainn*).

Ballynahow, the town of the river (*abh*).

Ballynakill (also **Ballynakilla**, **Ballynakilly**), the town of the church or wood (*cill* or *coill*).

Ballynalacken, the town of the *leacan* or hill side.

Ballynamona, the town of the bog (*móin*).

Ballynamuck, the town of the pigs (*muc*).

Ballynamuddagh, *Baile-na-mbodach*, the town of the *bodachs* or churls.

Ballynaraha, the town of the rath or fort.

Ballynatona (also **Ballynatone**), the town of the *backside* or hill (*tóin*).

Ballynatray, the town of the strand (*traigh*).

Ballyneety, *Baile-an-Fhaeite*, the town of White, a family name of English origin.

Ballyness, the town of the waterfall (*eas*).

Ballynew (also **Ballynoe**), *Baile-nua*, new town.

Ballynure, *Baile-an-iubhair*, the town of the yew.

Ballyorgan, in Limerick: Organ's or Horgan's town.

Ballyragget, in Kilkenny: *Bel-atha-Raghat*, F.M., Ragat's ford-mouth.

Ballyroe, *Baile-ruadh*, red town.

Ballyroosky, the town of the *rusk* or marsh.

Ballysadare, in Sligo: originally *Eas-dara* (Assdara), the cataract of the oak, from the beautiful fall on the Owenmore river. It was afterwards called *Baile-easa-dara* (Ballyassadara), F.M., the town of Assdara, which has been shortened to the present name.

Ballysaggart, the town of the *sagart* or priest.

Ballysakeery, in Mayo. *See* page 9.

Ballysallagh, dirty town.

Ballyshane, Shane's or John's town.

Ballyshannon: the old ford on the Erne is called by the annalists *Ath-seanaigh* and *Bel-atha-seanaigh* (Bellashanny). From the latter the present name is derived and it means the mouth of *Seanach's* or *Shannagh's* ford, a man's name in common use. The *on* is a modern corruption. The peasantry call the town *Ballyshanny*, which is nearer the original. Ballyshannon in Kildare is similarly derived.

Ballytarsna (also **Ballytarsney**), cross-town, i.e. the village or townland had a *cross* or transverse position.

Ballyteige, O'Teige's town.

Ballytrasna, *see* Ballytarsna.

Ballyvaghan, in Clare: *Baile-ui-Bheachain*, O'Behan's town.

Ballywater, *Baile-uachtar*, upper town.

Ballywillin, the town of the mill (*muileann*).

Balrath, *Baile-ratha*, the town of the fort.

Balrathboyne, in Meath: St Baeithin (Bweeheen, but often pronounced Boyne), the son of *Cuana*, built a church here near an ancient rath and the rath remains though the church is gone. Hence it was called *Rath-Baeithin*, and in recent times, Balrathboyne, the town of *Baeithin's* rath.

Balrothery, *Baile-a'-ridire* (Ballyariddery), the town of the knight.

Baltinglass, written *Bealach-Chonglais* (Ballaconglas) in Irish authorities, the road or pass of *Cuglas*, a person about whom there is a very ancient legend.

Baltrasna, *see* Ballytarsna.

Baltray, the town of the strand (*traigh*).

Banagh, barony of, in Donegal. It is called in the annals *Baghaineach* (Bawnagh), i.e. the territory of *Boghaine* (Boana) or *Enna Boghaine*, the son of Conall Gulban, son of the great king Niall of the Nine Hostages, who reigned from AD 379 to 405.

Banagher (also **Bangor**), *Beannchor* (Banaher), F.M., (from the root *beann*), signifies horns or pointed hills or rocks and sometimes simply a pointed hill.

Bannow, in Wexford: the harbour was called *Cuan-an-bhainbh* (Coon-an-wonniv), the harbour of the *bonniv* or sucking pig and the village has preserved the latter part of the name changed to Bannow.

Bansha, *Bainseach* (Bawnsha), a level place.

Bantry, *Beantraighe* (Bantry), Book of R., i.e. the descendants of *Beann* (Ban), one of the sons of Conor Mac Nessa, king of Ulster in the first century. A part of the tribe settled in Wexford and another part in Cork, and the barony of Bantry in the former county and the town of Bantry in the latter retain their name.

Barna, *Bearna*, a gap.

Barnaboy, yellow gap.

Barnageeha (also **Barnageehy**), windy gap (*gaoth*).

Barnane Ely, in Tipperary: from the remarkable gap in the Devil's Bit mountain *Bearnán-Eile*, the little gap of Ely, the ancient territory in which it was situated.

Barnes (also **Barnish**), *Bearnas*, a gap.

Barnismore, great gap.

Barr, the top of anything.

Baslick, *Baisleac*, F.M., a *basilica* or church.

Batterstown, the town of the *batter* (*bóthar*) or road.

Bawnmore, great green field.

Bawnoge, little green field.

Bawnreagh, greyish green field.

Baunskeha, the green field of the bush (*sceach*).

Bawnboy, yellow field.

Bawnfune, *Bán-fionn*, white field.

Bawnmore, great green field.

Beagh, *Beitheach* (Beha), a place of birches.

Bear, barony, island and haven in Cork. Owen More, king of Munster in the second century, spent nine years in Spain and, according to an old legend, he married *Beara*, daughter of the king of the country. On his return to Ireland to make war against Conn of the Hundred Battles, he landed on the north side of Bantry Bay and called the place *Beara* in honour of his wife.

Beheenagh (also **Behernagh**), a place of birches (*beith*).

Behy, birch land.

Belfarsad, *see* **Belfast**.

Belfast In old times the Lagan used to be crossed here by a *farset* or sandbank and hence the place was called *Belfeirste*, F.M., the *bel* or ford of the *farset*.

Bellaghy, the mouth or entrance of the *lahagh* or slough.

Bellanacargy, in Cavan: *Bel-atha-na-cairrge*, the mouth of the ford of the rock (*carraig*).

Bellanagher, in Roscommon: *Bel-atha-na-gcarr*, the mouth of the ford of the cars.

Bellananagh, in Cavan: *Bel-atha-na-neach*, the mouth of the ford of the horses (*each*).

Bellaugh, in Roscommon: *see* **Bellaghy**.

Belleek, near Ballyshannon: *Bel-leice* (**Bellecka**), F.M., the ford-mouth of the flag stone, from the flat surfaced rock in the bed of the river. Belleek in other places is similarly derived.

Beltany, from *Bealtaine* or *Beltaine*, the first of May, because the May day sports used to be celebrated there.

Ben, a peak, a pointed hill (*beann*).

Benbo mountain near Manorhamilton is called in Irish *Beanna-bo*, F.M., the peaks or horns of the cow from its curious double peak.

Benburb, in Tyrone: from a cliff over the Blackwater, called in the annals *Beann-borb*, the proud peak.

Bengore Head, the peak of the goats (*gabhar*).

Bengorm, blue peak.

Benmore, great peak.

Bignion (also **Binnion**), small *ben* or peak.

Billy, in Antrim: *bile* an ancient tree.

Binbulbin, correct name *Binn-Gulbain*, Gulban's peak.

Bogagh (also **Boggagh**, **Boggan**, **Boggaun**), a boggy place.

Boher, *Bothar* (boher), a road.

Boherard, high road.

Boherboy, yellow road.

Boherduff, *see* page 7.

Bohereen, little road.

Bohermeen, smooth road.

Boherroe, red road.

Boho, in Fermanagh: *Botha* (boha), tents or huts.

Bohola, *Both-Thola*, Hy. F., *St Tola's* hut.

Boley, *buaile*, a milking or dairy place.

Boleybeg, little *boley* or dairy place.

Boola, booley, *see* Boley.

Boolyglass, green *booley*.

Booterstown, near Dublin: the town of the *bothar*, *batter*, or road. In a roll of the fifteenth century it is called *Ballybothyr*, which shows that the Irish name was *Baile-an-bhothair*, the town of the road, of which the present name is a kind of half-translation.

Borheen, *see* **Bohereen**.

Borris, *Buirghes* (burris), a *burgage* or borough.

Borris-in-Ossory, from the old territory of Ossory.

Borrisokane, O'Keane's borough town.

Borrisoleigh, from the ancient territory *Ui Luighdheach* (Hy Leea), in which it was situated.

Bourney, in Tipperary: *Boirne* (bourny), rocky lands, the plural of *Burren*.

Bovevagh, *Both-Mheidhbhe* (Boh-veva), the hut or tent of Maev or Mabel, a woman's name.

Boylagh, barony of, in Donegal: i.e. the territory of the O'Boyles.

Boyounagh, yellow *ounagh* or marsh (*abhnach*).

Braade, *see* **Braid**.

Brackagh (also **Brackenagh**, **Brackernagh**, **Bracklagh**), a speckled place, from *breac*, speckled.

Bracklin (also **Brackloon**), *Breac-cluain*, speckled meadow.

Braid, The, in Antrim: applied to the deep glen through which the river flows. *Braghad* (braud), a gullet or gorge.

Brandon hill in Kerry, and also in Kilkenny: both called from St Brendan the Navigator who flourished in the sixth century.

Bray, in Wicklow: it is called Bree in old documents and it took name from the rocky head near it: *Bri* (bree), a hill. The name of Bray head in Valentia Island in Kerry is similarly derived.

Breaghva (also **Breaghwy**, **Breaghy**), *Breach-mhagh* (Brea-vah), the plain of the wolves (*breach*, a wolf; *magh*, a plain).

Breandrum, stinking *drum* or ridge.

Brigown, near Mitchelstown in Cork: written *Bri-gobh-unn* (Breegown) in the Book of Lismore, the *bree* or hill of the smith (*gobha*).

Brittas, speckled land.

Britway, in Cork: *see* **Breaghva**.

Brockagh, a place of *brocs* or badgers.

Bruff, in Limerick: a corrupt form of *Brugh* (bru), a fort or mansion. The *brugh* is the old fort near the town.

Bruis, another form of *Brugh* (bru), a mansion.

Bruree, in Limerick: called in Irish documents *Brugh-righ* (Bruree), the fort or palace of the king, for it was the chief seat of Olioll Olum, king of Munster in the second century, and afterwards of the O'Donovans. Several of the old forts still remain.

Bullaun, *Bullán*, a wall in a rock.

Bun, the bottom or end of anything; the mouth of a river.

Buncrana, the mouth of the river Crana.

Bunlahy, the end of the *lahagh* or slough.

Bunratty, in Clare: the mouth of the river Ratty, now called the Owen O'Garney.

Burren, *Boireann*, a rock, a rocky district.

Burriscara, the *burris* or borough of the old territory of Carra.

Burrishoole, derived like Burriscarra, from the territory of *Umhall* (ool) or 'The Owles'.

Burrisnafarney, in Tipperary: the *burris* or borough of the alder-plain (*see* **Farney**).

Buttevant, in Cork: from the French motto of the Barrys, *Boutez-en-avant*, push forward. The Irish name is Kilnamullagh, the *cell* or church of the summits (*mullach*).

Cliffs of Moher, Co. Clare

Cabragh, bad land.

Caher, *cathair* (caher), a circular stone fort.

Caherbarnagh, gapped *caher* or fort: *bearnach*, gapped.

Caherconlish, in Limerick: *Cathair-chinn-lis*, the *caher* at the head of the *lis* or fort.

Caherduggan, Duggan's *caher* or stone fort.

Cahergal, white *caher* or stone fort.

Caherkeen, in Cork: beautiful *caher* or fort.

Cahersiveen, in Kerry: it exactly preserves the pronunciation of the Irish name *Cathair-Saidhbhín*, the stone fort of *Saidhbhín*, or Sabina, a woman's name.

Cahirconree mountain, near Tralee: *Curoi's* caher, i.e. the celebrated chief, *Curoi Mac Daire*, who flourished in the first century. His caher still remains on a shoulder of the mountain.

Caldragh, *Cealdrach*, an old burying ground.

Callow, *Cala*, a marshy meadow along a river.

Callowhill, *Callchoill*, hazel wood (*coll* and *coill*).

Caltragh, *see* Caldragh.

Calluragh, *Ceallurach*, an old burial ground.

Camas (also Camus), anything that winds, a winding stream, from *cam*, crooked.

Camlin, crooked line. Often applied to a river.

Camlough, crooked lake (*cam* and *loch*).

Cappa (also Cappagh), *ceapach*, a plot of land laid down for tillage.

Cappaghbeg, little tillage-plot.

Cappaghmore (also Cappamore), great tillage-plot.

Cappaghwhite, in Tipperary, White's tillage-plot.

Capparoe, red plot.

Cappog (also Cappoge), little *cappagh* or plot.

Cappoquin, *Ceapach-Chuinn*, Conn's tillage-plot.

Caran (also Caraun), a rocky place (from *carr*).

Carbury baronies, in Longford and Sligo: so called because they were inhabited by the descendants of Carbery, one of the sons of Niall of the Nine Hostages, king of Ireland from AD 379 to 405.

Cargagh, a rock place (from *carraig*).

Cargan (also Cargin), a little rock, a rocky place.

Carha, *Cairthe* (carha), a pillar stone.

Carhoo, *ceathramhadh* (carhoo), a quarter (of land).

Carlingford, *ford* is the Danish *fiord*, a sea inlet. The old Irish name is *Cairlinn*: Carlingford, the *fiord* of *Cairlinn*.

Carlow, called in Irish documents *Cetherloch* (Cahorlough), quadruple lake (*cether*, four); the Barrow anciently formed four lakes there.

Carn, a monumental heap of stones.

Carnacally, the carn of the hag (*cailleach*).

Carnalbanagh, the carn of the *Albanach* or Scotsman.

Carnaun, little carn or monumental heap.

Carnbane, white carn (*ban* (bawn), white).

Carndonagh, in Innishowen: so called because the carn was situated in the parish of Donagh.

Carnew, *Carn-Naoi* (Nee), Naoi's carn.

Carnglass, green carn.

Carnlough, the carn of the lake.

Carnmore, great carn.

Carnsore Point The old Irish name is *carn*, a monumental heap; the termination *ore* is Danish and signifies the sandy point of a promontory: Carnsore is merely Carn's *ore*, the *ore* or sandy point of the carn.

Carnteel, in Tyrone: *Carn-tSiadhail* (Carn-teel), F.M., *Siadhal's* or Shiel's carn (*s* eclipsed).

Carn Tierna, near Fermoy. *Tighernach* (Tierna), *Tetbannach*, king of Munster in the first century, was buried under the great carn which still remains on the top of the hill; and hence the name signifying Tierna's carn.

Carntogher hills in Londonderry: the carn of the *togher* or causeway.

Carrantuohill, the highest mountain in Ireland. It descends on the Killarney side by a curved edge which the spectator catches in profile, all jagged and serrated with great masses of rock projecting like teeth. *Tuathail* (thoohil) means left-handed and is applied to anything reversed from its proper direction; *carrán* is a reaping hook; and Carrantuohill is 'the reversed reaping hook' because the teeth are on a convex instead of a concave edge.

Carrick, a rock, Irish *carraig* (carrig).

Carrickbeg, little rock.

Carrickduff, black rock.

Carrickfergus, Fergus's rock.

Carrickmore, great rock.

Carrick-on-Shannon Carrick is here a corruption of *carra*, a weir; and the place took its name from an ancient weir across the Shannon. Its old anglicised name was Carrickdrumrusk, properly Carra-Drumrusk, the weir of Drumrusk.

Carrick-on-Suir, the rock of the Suir; from a large rock in the bed of the river.

Carrig, a rock, *see* Carrick.

Carrigafoyle, on the Shannon near Ballylongford: *Carraig-a'-phoill*, the rock of the hole; from a deep hole in the river, near the castle.

Carrigaholt, in Clare: written by the F.M., *Carraigh-an-chobhlaigh* (Carrigahowly), the rock of the fleet; and it took its name from the rock which rises over the bay where the fleets anchored. The local pronunciation of the Irish name is Carrigaholty, from which the present name is derived. Another place of the same name which preserves the correct pronunciation is Carrigahowly on Newport bay in Mayo, the castle of the celebrated Grace O'Malley.

Carrigaline, in Cork: the rock of O'Lehane.

Carrigallen, in Leitrim: *Carraig-áluinn*, beautiful rock; from the rock on which the original church was built.

44

Carrigan (also **Carrigane**), little rock.

Carrigans, little rocks.

Carrigdownane, Downan's or Downing's rock.

Carrigeen, little rock: **Carrigeens**, little rocks.

Carrignavar, in Cork: *see page 8.*

Carrigogunnell, near the Shannon in Limerick: *Carraig-O-gCoinneli*, F.M., the rock of the O'Connells.

Carrigroe, red rock.

Carrow, a quarter (of land). *See* Carhoo.

Carroward, high quarter-land.

Carrowbane (also **Carrowbaun**), white quarter-land.

Carrowbeg, little quarter-land.

Carrowcrin, the quarter-land of the tree (*crann*).

Carrowduff, black quarter-land.

Carrowgarriff (also **Carrowgarve**), rough quarter (*garbh*, rough).

Carrowkeel, narrow quarter (*cael*, narrow).

Carrowmanagh, middle quarter-land.

Carrowmore, great quarter-land.

Carrownaglogh, the quarter of the stones (*cloch*).

Carrownamaddoo (also **Carrownamaddra**, **Carrownamaddy**), the quarter of the dogs (*madadh*, and *madradh*).

Carrowntober, the quarter-land of the well (*tober*).

Carrowreagh (also **Carrowrevagh**), grey quarter (*riabhach*).

Carrowroe, red quarter-land.

Cartron, an Anglo-Norman word, meaning a quarter of land.

Cashel all the places of this name, including Cashel in Tipperary, were so called from a *caiseal* (cashel) or circular stone fort.

Cashen river, *casán* a path: for this river was, as it were, the high road into Kerry.

Cashlan, *Caislen*, a castle.

Castlebane (also **Castlebaun**), white castle.

Castlebar, in Mayo: shortened from Castle-Barry for it belonged to the Barrys after the English invasion.

Castlecomer, the castle of the river-confluence (*comar*).

Castleconnell, near Limerick: *see page 9.*

Castledermot, in Kildare: the old name was Disertdermot, Diarmad's *desert* or hermitage, from Diarmad, son of the King of Ulidia who founded a monastery there about AD800. The present form of the name is derived from a castle built there by Walter de Riddlesford in the time of Strongbow.

Castledillon, in Kildare: Irish name *Disert-Iolladhan* (Disertillan), *Iolladhan's* or Illan's hermitage; and the word Castle was substituted for Disert as in the last name.

Castlelyons, in Cork: the castle of O'Lehane or Lyons.

Castlemoyle, bald or dilapidated castle (*mael*).

Castlepook, the castle of the *pooka* or sprite.

Castlerahan, the castle of the little rath or fort.

Castlereagh, grey caste (*riabhach*).

Castleterra, in Cavan: a corruption from the Irish *Cos-a'-tsiorraigh* (Cussatirry), the foot (*cos*) of the *searrach* or foal. The name is accounted for by a legend about a stone with the print of a colt's foot on it.

Castleventry, in Cork: the Irish name is *Caislean-na-gaeithe* (Cashlaunnageeha), the castle of the wind, of which the present name is a kind of translation.

Cavan, *Cabhan*, a hollow place. In some parts of Ulster it is understood to mean a hard round hill.

Cavanacaw, the round hill of the chaff (*cáth*); from the practice of winnowing.

Cavanaleck, the hill of the flag-stone.

Cavanreagh, grey hill (*riabhach* (reagh) grey).

Celbridge, in Kildare, the *cell*, *kill* or church of the bridge; a kind of half-translation from the original Irish name *Cill-droichid* (Kildrohed), the church of the *drohed* or bridge which is still retained as the name of the parish but shortened to Kildrought.

Cheek Point, on the Suir below Waterford: a corruption of *Sheega* Point, the Irish name being *Poínte-na-síge*, the point of the *sheegas* or fairies.

Claggan, *Claigeann*, the skull, a round hill.

Clankee, barony of, in Cavan: *Clann-an-chaoich* (Clann-an-kee), the *clan* or descendants of the one-eyed man. They derived this cognomen from Niall O'Reilly, slain in 1256, who was called *caech* (kee), i.e. one-eyed.

Clanmaurice, barony of, in Kerry: the *clan* or descendants of Maurice Fitzgerald.

Clanwilliam, baronies of, in Limerick and Tipperary: the *clan* or descendants of William Burke.

Clara (also **Claragh**), a level place; from *clar*.

Clare, a level piece of land (*clar*).

Clareen, little *clar* or level plain.

Clare-Galway Irish name *Baile-an-chlair* (Ballinclare), F.M., the town of the plain; of which only the latter part is retained: called Clare-Galway to distinguish it from other Clares.

Clash, *Clais*, a trench or furrow.

Clashduff, black trench.

Clashganniff (Clashganniv, Clashganny), the trench of the sand, i.e. a sandpit (*gainimh* (ganniv), sand).

Clashmore, great trench.

Cleenish, *Claen-inis* (Cleeninish), sloping *inis* or island.

Cleggan, *see* Claggan.

Clifden, in Galway: a very modern corruption of the Irish name *Clochán*, which signifies a beehive-shaped stone house.

Cliffs of Moher The term *Mothar* (Moher) is applied in the south of Ireland to the ruin of a *caher*, *rath* or fort; and on a cliff near Hag's Head there stands an old stone fort called Moher O'Ruan, O'Ruan's ruined fort, from which the cliffs of Moher received their name.

Clogh, a stone; often applied also to a stony castle.

Cloghan (also **Cloghane**, **Cloghaun**), a row of stepping stones across a river (from *cloch*).

Cloghbally, stony *bally* or townland.

Cloghboley (also **Cloghboola**), stony *booley* or dairy place.

Cloghbrack, speckled stone.

Cloghcor, rough stone.

Clogheen, little stone or stone castle.

Clogher, generally applied to stony land – a place full of stones; but occasionally it means a rock.

Clogherbrien, in Kerry: *Braen's* stony place.

Cloghereen, a place full of stones (*cloch*).

Cloghernagh (also **Clogherny**), a stony place.

Cloghfin, *Cloch-finn*, white stone.

Cloghineely, in Donegal: *Cloch-Chinnfhaelaidh* (Clogh-Kineely), F.M.,

Kineely's or Mac Kineely's stone. Name accounted for by a long legend. The stone which gave name to the district is still preserved.

Cloghoge, a stony place.

Cloghpook, the *pooka's* or sprite's stone.

Cloghran, *Cloichréan*, a stony place.

Cloghvoley (also **Cloghvoola**, **Cloghvoolia**, **Cloghvoula**), *Cloch-bhuaile*, stony *booley* or dairy place.

Cloghy, a stony place.

Clogrennan, *Cloch-grianáin*, the stone castle of the *grianan* or summer residence.

Clomantagh, in Kilkenny: Mantagh's stone castle.

Clon, a meadow. *See* Cloon.

Clonad, *Cluain-fhada* (Cloonada), long meadow.

Clonagh, *Cluain-each*, horse meadow.

Clonallan, in Down: called by Colgan and others *Cluain-Dallain*, Dallan's meadow; from Dallan Forgall, a celebrated poet of the sixth century.

Clonalvy, *Cluain-Ailbhe*, Ailbhe's or Alvy's meadow.

Clonamery, the meadow of the *iomaire* or ridge.

Clonard, in Meath: written in Irish authorities *Cluain-Eraird*, Erard's meadow. There are several other places called Clonard and Cloonard; but in these the Irish form is probably *Cluain-ard*, high meadow.

Clonarney, *Cluain-airne*, the meadow of sloes.

Clonaslee, the meadow of the *slighe* (slee) or road.

Clonbeg, little meadow.

Clonbrock, the meadow of the *brocs* or badgers.

Cloncrew, in Limerick: *Cluain-creamha* (crawa), the meadow of wild garlic.

Cloncullen, holly meadow.

Cloncurry, shortened from *Cluain-Conaire* (Cloon-Conary), F.M., Conary's meadow.

Clondalkin, near Dublin: *Cluain-Dolcain*, Dolcan's meadow.

Clonduff, in Down: *Cluain-daimh* (dav), O'C. Cal., the meadow of the ox.

Clone, a meadow: *see* Clon and Cloon.

Cloneen, little meadow.

Clonegall, in Carlow: *Cluain-na-nGall* (Cloon-nung-aul), the meadow of the *Galls* or foreigners.

Clonenagh, in Laois: *Cluain-eidhnech* (enagh), O'C. Cal., the meadow of ivy (see *Eidhneán* in Irish Root Words). It was so called before the sixth century and to this day it abounds in ivy.

Clones (pronounced in two syllables), *Cluain-Eois* (Cloonoce), F.M., the meadow of *Eos* (Oce), a man's name.

Clonfad (also **Clonfadda** and **Cloonfad**), *Cluain-fada*, long meadow.

Clonfeacle, in Tyrone: called *Cluain-fiacla* (feckla) in the Book of Leinster; the meadow of the tooth.

Clonfert, the Book of Leinster writes the name *Cluain-ferta*, the meadow of the grave.

Clongill, *Cluain-Gaill*, the meadow of the foreigner.

Clongowes, the meadow of the smith (*gobha*).

Clonkeen, *Cluain-caein* (keen), beautiful meadow.

Clonlea (also **Clonleigh** and **Cloonlee**), *Cluain-laegh* (lee), the meadow of the calves.

Clonliff, the meadow of herbs (*lubh*, a herb).

Clonmacnoise, written in Irish documents of the eighth century *Cluain-maccu-Nois*, which was the old pagan name: it signifies the meadow of the sons of *Nos*. This *Nos* was the son of *Fiadhach* (Feeagh), a chief of the tribe of *Dealbhna* or Devlin in whose territory Clonmacnoise was situated.

Clonmeen, *Cluain-mín* (meen), smooth meadow.

Clonmel, *Cluain-meala* (malla), the meadow of honey (*mil*).

Clonmellon, *Cluain-milain*, F.M., Milian's meadow.

Clonmelsh, *Cluain-milis*, sweet meadow (from honey).

Clonmore, great meadow.

Clonmult, the meadow of the wethers (*molt*).

Clonoghil, the meadow of the yew-wood (*eóchaill*).

Clonoulty, *Cluain-Ultaigh* (ulty), the Ulsterman's meadow.

Clonshire, *Cluain-siar*, western meadow.

Clonsillá, *Cluain-saileach*, the meadow of sallows.

Clonskeagh, *Cluain-sceach*, the meadow of the white thorns.

Clontarf, *Clain-tarbh* (tarriv), F.M., the meadow of the bulls.

Clontibret, written by the annalists *Cluain-tiobrat*, the meadow of the spring (*tipra*, same as *tobar*).

Clonturk (also **Cloonturk**), the boar's meadow (*torc*).

Clonty, *see* Cloonty.

Clonygowan, *Cluain-na-ngamhan* (Cloon-nung-own), F.M., the meadow of the calves.

Clonyhurk, *Cluain-da-thorc* (Cloonahork), F.M., the meadow of the two boars.

Cloon (also **Cloone**), a meadow. See *Cluain* in vocabulary.

Cloonagh, the meadow of horses (*each*).

Cloonard, *see* Clonard.

Cloonawillin, *Cluain-a'-mhuilinn*, the meadow of the mill.

Cloonbeg, little meadow.

Clooncah, the meadow of the battle (*cath*).

Clooncoose (also **Clooncose**), *Cluain-cuas*, F.M., the meadow of the caves.

Clooncraff, *see* Cloncrew.

Clooncunna (Clooncunnig, Clooncuny), the meadow of the firewood (*conadh*).

Cloondara, *Cluain-da-rath*, F.M., the meadow of the two raths or forts.

Cloonee (also **Clooney**), meadow land.

Clooneen, little meadow.

Cloonfinlough, the meadow of the clear lake.

Cloonkeen, *Cluain-caein*, beautiful meadow.

Cloonlara, the meadow of the mare (*lárach*).

Cloonlougher, the meadow of the rushes (*luachra*).

Cloonmore, great meadow.

Cloonnagashel, in Mayo. *See* page 8.

Cloonshannagh (also **Cloonshinnagh**), fox meadow (*sionnach*).

Cloonshee, the meadow of the fairies (*sidh*).

Cloonsillagh, the meadow of the sallows.

Cloonteen, little meadow.

Cloonties, *Cluainte*, meadows (English plural form).

Cloontubbrid, *see* Clontibret.

Cloontuskert, *Cluain-tuaisceirt* (tooskert), F.M., northern meadow.

Cloonty, *Cluainte*, meadows, plural of *cluain*.

Cloran, (also **Clorane**, **Clorhane**), a stony place (*cloch*).

Clough, a stone or stone castle.

Cloyne, in Cork: shortened from *Cluain-uamha* (Cloonooa), as it is written in the Book of Leinster. The name signifies the meadow of the cave (*uaimh*); and the cave is still to be seen.

Clyduff, black dyke or mound (*cladh*).

Colehill, *Coll-choill*, hazel wood.

Coleraine We are told in the Tripartite Life of St Patrick that a chieftain named Nadslua presented the saint with a piece of land on the bank of the river Bann on which to build a church. It was a spot overgrown with ferns and it happened at the moment that some boys were amusing themselves by setting them on fire. Hence the place was called *Cuil-rathain* (Coolrahen) which Colgan translates *Secessus filicis*, the corner (*cuil*) of the ferns. Coolraine, Coolrainey and Coolrahnee are similarly derived.

Collon, a place of hazels (*coll*).

Colp, near Drogheda. According to an ancient legend, when the Milesian brothers invaded Ireland, one of them, Colpa the swordsman, was drowned at the mouth of the Boyne; hence it was called Inver-Colpa. Colpa's river mouth; and the parish of Colp on its southern bank retains the latter part of the name a little shortened.

Comber (also **Comer**), see page 10.

Commaun, a little *cum* or hollow.

Conicar (also **Conicker**, **Conigar**, **Coneykeare**), *Cuinicér* (cunnikere), a rabbit warren.

Conlig, the *liag* or stone of the hounds (*cu*).

Connello, baronies of, in Limerick. This was the ancient territory of the tribe of Hy Conall or *Hy Conaill Gabra* (Goura) (so written in the Book of Leinster) who were descended and named from Conall, the ninth in descent from Olioll Olum, king of Munster in the second century.

Connemara Maev, queen of Connaught in the time of Conor mac Nessa, had three sons by Fergus mac Roy, ex-king of Ulster, namely *Ciar* (Keer), *Conmac* and *Modhruadh* (Moroo). The descendants of *Conmac* were called *Conmacne* (*ne*, a progeny), and they were settled in Connaught, where they gave name to several territories. One of these, viz. the district lying west of Lough Corrib and Lough Mask, from its situation near the sea, was called, to distinguish it from the others, *Conmacne-mara* (O'Dugan: *muir*, the sea, gen. *mara*), or the sea-side *Conmacne*, which has been shortened to the present name Connemara.

Connor, in Antrim: written *Condeire* or *Condaire* in various authorities; the *derry* or oak wood of the dogs (*cu*), or as it is explained in a gloss in the Martyrology of Aengus, 'The oak wood in which were wild dogs formerly and she-wolves used to dwell therein.'

Convoy (also **Conva**), *Con-mhagh*, hound plain (*cu* and *magh*).

Conwal, *Congbhail* (Congwal), F.M., a habitation.

Cooga (also **Coogue**), *Coigeadh* (Coga), a fifth part.

Cool (also **Coole**), *cuil*, a corner or *cul*, a back.

Coolattin, the corner of the furze (*aiteann*).

Coolavin, a barony in Sligo: *Cuil-O'bhFinn* (Coolovin): F.M., the corner or angle of the O'Finns.

Coolbanagher, the angle of the pinnacles (*see* Banagher).

Coolbane (also **Coolbaun**), white corner or back.

Coolcashin, Cashin's corner or angle.

Coolderry, back *derry* or oak wood.

Cooleen, little corner; **Cooleeny**, little corners.

Cooleeshal (also **Coolishal**), low corner (*íseal*).

Cooley hills, near Carlingford. After the defeat of the Tuatha de Danaan by the Milesians at Teltown in Meath, the Milesian chief *Cuailgne* (Cooley), following up the pursuit, was slain here; and the district was called from him, *Cuailgne*, which name is still applied to the range of hills.

Coolgreany, sunny corner or back (*grian*, the sun).

Coolhill (also **Coolkill**), *cúl-choill*, back wood.

Coolnahinch, the corner of the *inis*, island, or river meadow.

Coolock (also **Coologe**), little corner or angle.

Coolroe, red corner or back.

Coom (also **Coombe**), *cúm*, a hollow or mountain valley.

Coomnagoppul, at Killarney: *Cúm-na-gcapall*, the hollow or valley of the horses; from the practice of sending horses to graze in it.

Coomyduff, near Killarney: *Cúm-ui-Dhuibh* (Coomywiv), O'Duff's valley; usually but erroneously translated Black valley.

Coos (also **Coose**), *cuas*, a cave.

Coosan (also **Coosane**, **Coosaun**), little cave.

Cor (also **Corr**), several meanings but generally signifies a round hill.

Corballis (also **Corbally**), odd townland: *cor* here means odd.

Corbeagh, round hill of the birch (*beith*).

Corcomohide, in Limerick: *Corca-Muichet* (Book of Lismore), the race (*corca*) of *Muichet*, one of the disciples of the druid *Mogh Ruith*.

Corcomroe, barony of, in Clare: *Corca-Modhruadh* or *Corcomruadh* (Corcomrua: Book of Leinster), the race (*corca*) of *Modhruadh*, son of queen Maev. (*See* Connemara.)

Corcreevy, branchy hill. *Craebh* (creeve), a branch.

Cordangan, fortified *cor* or round hill.

Cordarragh, round hill of the oak (*dair*).

Corduff, black round hill.

Corgarve, rough round hill (*garbh*).

Corglass, green round hill (*glas*).

Corick, the meeting of two rivers.

Cork, *Corcach*, a marsh. The city grew round a monastery founded in the sixth century on the edge of a marsh by St Finbar; and even yet a part of the city is called the Marsh.

Corkagh, *see* Cork.

Corkaguiny, barony of, in Kerry: *Corca-Duibhne* (divny: O'Dugan), the race (*corca*) of *Duibhne*, son of Carbery Musc who was son of Conary II, king of Ireland from AD 158 to 165. *D* changed to *g*: *see* page 10.

Corkaree, barony of, in Westmeath: *Corca Raeidhe* (Ree: O'Dugan), the race (*corca*) of *Fiacha Raidhe* (Feeha Ree), grandson of Felimy the Lawgiver, king of Ireland from AD 111 to 119.

Corkeeran (also **Corakeeran**), the round hill of the *keerans* or quicken trees (*caerthainn*).

Corkey, *see* Cork.

Corlat, the round hill of the sepulchres (*leacht*).

Corlea, grey round hill.

Corlough, the lake of the *corrs* or herons.

Cormeen, smooth round hill.

Cornacreeve, the round hill of the branchy tree (*craebh*).

Cornagee (also **Cornageeha**), the round hill of the wind (*gaeth*).

Cornahoe, the round hill of the cave (*uaimh*).

Cornamucklagh, the round hill of the piggeries. See Mucklagh.

Cornaveagh, the round hills of the ravens (*fiach*).

Corratober, the round hill of the well (*tobar*).

Corrinshigo (also **Corrinshigagh**), the round hill of the ash trees. See

Fuinnse in Irish Root Words.

Corrofin, in Clare: *Coradh-Finne* (Corrafinna), F.M., the weir of Finna, a woman's name.

Corskeagh, the round hill of the white thorns.

Coshbride (also **Coshlea**, **Coshma**), baronies, the first in Waterford, the others in Limerick. Cosh (*cois*, from *cos* a foot), means at the foot of, near, beside. Coshbride, the barony along the river Bride. Cosh-lea, *cois-shleibhe* (cushleva), at the foot of the *sliabh* or mountain, i.e. the Galtees. **Coshma**, *Cois-Maighe* (ma), the barony along the river Maigue.

Craan (also **Cranne**), a stony place (from *carr*).

Crag (also **Craig**), other forms of *carraig*, a rock.

Cran, *Crann*, a tree.

Cranfield, a corruption of *Creamh-choill* (Cravwhill), the wood (*coill*) of wild garlic (*creamh*).

Crannagh, a place abounding in *cranns* or trees.

Crannoge, a habitation on an artificial island in a lake.

Cranny, *see* Crannagh.

Cratloe (also **Crataloe**), sallow wood.

Craughwell, *Creamh-choill*, wild garlic wood.

Crecora, in Limerick: *Craebh-cumhraidhe* (Crave-coory). (O'Dugan) sweet scented *creeve* or branchy tree.

Creevagh, a branchy place (*craebh*).

Creeve, *Craebh* (creeve), a branch or branchy tree.

Creevelea, grey branch or branchy tree.

Creevy, *see* Creevagh.

Creg (also **Cregg**), *creag*, a rock.

Creggan (also **Creggane**, **Creggaun**), little rock, rocky ground.

Cremorne barony, in Monaghan: *Crioch-Mughdhorn* (Cree-Mourne), the country (*crioch*) of the tribe of *Mughdhorna* (Mourna), who were descended and named from *Mughdhorn* (Mourne), the son of Colla Meann, one of the three brothers who conquered Ulster, and destroyed the palace of Emania in AD 332.

Crew, *see* Creeve.

Croagh, *Cruach*, a rick or stacked up hill.

Croaghan (also **Croaghaun**), a round or piled up hill.

Croaghpatrick, St Patrick's rick or hill.

Crock is very generally used in the northern half of Ireland instead of Knock, a hill.

Crockanure, *Cnoc-an-iúbhair*, the hill of the yew.

Crogh, *see* Croagh.

Croghan (also **Crohane**), *see* Croaghan.

Crossakeel, slender crosses.

Crossboyne, *Cros-Baeithin*, Hy F., *Baeithin's* or Boyne's cross.

Crosserlough, the cross on (*air*) or near the lake.

Crossgar, short cross.

Crossmaglen, in Armagh: *Cros-meg-Fhloinn* (Cros-meg-lin: *fh* silent), the cross of Flann's son.

Crossmolina, in Mayo: *Cros-ui-Mhaelfhina*, F.M., O'Mulleeny's or Mullany's cross.

Crossoge, little cross.

Crossreagh, grey cross (*reabhach*).

Cross, *Cruit*, a hump, a humpy backed hill.

Cruagh, *see* Croagh.

Cruit, *see* Cross.

Crumlin (also **Cromlin**), *Cruim-ghlinn* (Crumlin), F.M., curved glen.

Crusheen, *Croisin*, little cross.

Cuilbeg (also **Cuilmore**), little wood, great wood (*coill*).

Culdaff, *Cul-dabhach* (culdava), the back (*cul*) of the flax-dam or pool.

Culfeightrin, in Antrim: *Cuil-eachtrann* (Coolaghtran), the corner (*cuil*) of the strangers.

Cullan (also **Cullane**, **Cullaun**), a place of hazels (*coll*).

Culleen, *Coillín*, little wood.

Cullen, *Cuillionn* (Cullen), holly, holly land.

Cullenagh, a place producing holly.

Cullentra (also **Cullentragh**), *see* Cullenagh.

Cullenwaine, in Offaly: *Cuil-O-nDubhain* (Coolonuan), F.M., the corner or angle of the O'Duanes.

Cullion, *see* Cullen.

Cully, woodland; from *coill*.

Culmullen, in Meath: the angle of the mill.

Cumber (also **Cummer**). *See* page 10.

Curra (also **Curragh**), *currach*, generally a marsh; sometimes a race course.

Currabaha (also **Currabeha**), the marsh of the birch.

Curraghbeg, little marsh.

Curraghboy, yellow marsh.

Curraghduff, black marsh.

Curraghlahan (also **Curraghlan**), broad marsh.

Curraghmore, great marsh.

Curragh of Kildare. The word here means a race course: the Curragh of Kildare has been used as a race course from the earliest ages.

Curraheen, little *currach* or marsh.

Curry, another form of Curragh, a marsh.

Cush, *see* Coshbride.

Cushendall, in Antrim: *Cois-abhann-Dhalla* (Cush-oun-dalla), the foot or termination of the river Dall.

Cushendun, in Antrim: called by the F.M., *Bun-abhann-Duine*, the end, i.e. the mouth of the river Dun; this was afterwards changed to *Cois-abhan-Duine* (Cush-oun-Dunny) by the substitution of *Cois*, the foot or end for *Bun*.

Cutteen, *Coitchionn* (cutteen), a common, a commonage.

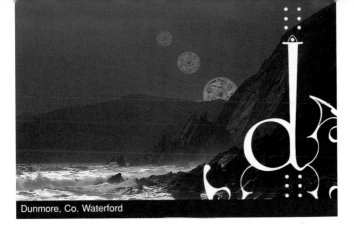
Dunmore, Co. Waterford

Dalkey Island near Dublin. The Irish name is *Delg-inis* (O'C. Cal.), thorn island; which the Danes, who had a fortress on it in the tenth century, translated to the present name by changing *Delg* into their word *Dalk*, a thorn; and substituting the northern word *ey*, an island, for *inis*.

Dangan, *Daingean* (dangan), a fortress.

Dangandargan, in Tipperary: Dargan's fortress.

Darragh, a place producing oaks (*dair*).

Darraragh (also **Darrery**), an oak forest, a place abounding in oaks (*Dairbhreach*).

Dawros, *Damhros*, the peninsula of oxen (*damh* and *ros*).

Deelis (also **Deelish**), *Duibh-lios* (Divlis), black *lis* or fort.

Delvin There were formerly seven tribes called *Dealbh-na* (Dalvana), descended and named from *Lughaidh Dealbhaeth* (Lewy Dalway) who was the son of *Cas mac Tail* (seventh in descent from Olioll Olum: see Connello), the ancestor of the Dalcassians of Thomond: *Dealbhna*, *i.e. Dealbhaeth's* descendants. None of these have perpetuated their name except one, viz. *Dealbhna mor*, or the great *Dealbhna*, from whom the barony of Delvin in Westmeath received its name.

Dernish (also **Derinch**, **Derinish**), oak island (*dair*).

Derrada (also **Derradd**), *Doire-fhada*, long oak grove.

Derragh, *see* Darragh.

Derreen, little *derry* or oak grove or wood.

Derreens (also **Derries**), oak groves.

Derry, *Doire* (Derry), an oak grove or wood.

Derryad (also **Derryadda**), *Doira-fhada*, long oak wood.

Derrybane (also **Derrybawn**), whitish oak wood.

Derrybeg, little oak wood.

Derrycreevy, the oak wood of the branchy tree.

Derrydorragh (also **Derrydorraghy**), dark oak wood (*dorcha*).

Derryduff, black oak wood.

Derryfadda, long oak wood.

Derrygarriff (also **Derrygarve**), rough oak wood (*garbh*).

Derrylahan (also **Derrylane**), broad oak wood (*leathan*).

Derrylea, grey oak wood.

Derrylough (also **Derryloughan**), the oak wood of the lake.

Derrymore, great oak wood.

Derrynahinch, the oak wood of the island or river meadow (*inis*).

Derrynane, in Kerry: *Doire-Fhionain* (Derry-Eenane: *fh* silent), the oak grove of St Finan Cam, a native of Corkaguiny, who flourished in the sixth century.

Derrynaseer, the oak grove of the *saers* or carpenters.

Derryvullan, in Fermanagh: *Doire-Maelain* (Derry-Velan: *m* aspirated), F.M., Maelan's oak grove.

Desert, *Disert*, a desert or hermitage.

Desertcreat, corrupted from *Disert-da-Chrioch* (Disert-a-cree), F.M., the hermitage of the two territories.

Desertegny, Egnagh's hermitage.

Desertmartin, Martin's hermitage.

Desertmore, great desert or hermitage.

Desertserges, in Cork: Saerghus's hermitage.

Devenish Island, in Lough Erne: *Daimhinis* (Davinish), F.M., the island of the oxen (*damh*).

Diamor, written in the Dinnseanchus, *Diamar*, i.e. a solitude.

Dingle, from Dingin, another form of *Daingean*, a fortress, by a change from *n* to *l* (see page 9). Called in the annals *Daingean-ui-Chuis*, now usually written Dingle-I-Coush, the fortress of O'Cush, the ancient proprietor.

Dinish (also **Deenish**), *Duibh-inis* (Divinish), black island.

Disert, *see* Desert.

Donabate, *Domhnach-a'-bhaid*, the church of the boat.

Donagh, *Domhnach* (Downagh), a church.

Donaghcloney, in Down: the church of the *cluain* or meadow.

Donaghcumper, in Kildare: the church of the *cummer* or confluence.

Donaghedy, in Tyrone: *Domhnach-Chaeide* (Donaheedy), the church of St Caidoc, a companion of St Columbanus.

Donaghmore, great church.

Donaghmoyne, in Monaghan: *Domhnach-Maighin*, the church of the little plain.

Donard, high *dun* or fort.

Donegal The Danes had a settlement there before the Anglo-Norman invasion and hence it was called *Dun-na-nGall* (Doonagall), the fortress of the *Galls* or foreigners.

Doneraile, in Cork: written in the Book of Lismore *Dun-air-aill*, the fortress on the cliff.

Donnybrook, *Domhnach-Broc*, St Broc's church.

Donnycarney, *Cearnach's* or Carney's church.

Donohill, the fortress of the yew wood (*eóchaill*).

Donore, *Dun-uabhair* (Dunoor), Г.М., the fort of pride.

Doogary, *Dubhdhoire* (Dooary), black derry or oak wood.

Doon, *Dún*, a fortress.

Doonan (also **Doonane**), little *dun* or fort.

Doonard, high fort.

Doonass, near Killaloe: *Dun-easa*, the fortress of the cataract, i.e. the great rapid on the Shannon.

Doonbeg, little fortress.

Dooneen, little fort.

Doonfeeny, the fort of Finna (a woman).

Doonisky (also **Dunisky**), the fort of the water (*uisge*).

Doonooney, Una's fort.

Douglas, *Dubh-ghlaise*, black stream.

Down, a form of *Dun*, a fortress.

Downings, *Dooneens* or little forts.

Downpatrick takes its name from the large entrenched *dun* near the cathedral. In the first century this fortress was the residence of a warrior of the Red Branch Knights, called *Celtchair*, or Keltar of the battles from whom it is called in Irish authorities Dunkeltar. By ecclesiastical writers it is commonly called *Dun-da-leth-glas*, the fortress of the two broken locks (*glas*) or fetters. This long name was afterwards shortened to *Dun* or Down, which was extended to the county. The name of St Patrick was added to commemorate his connexion with the place.

Downs, *duns* or forts.

Dreen, *Draeighean* (dreean), the blackthorn.

Dreenagh, a place producing blackthorns.

Dreenan, blackthorn, a place of blackthorns.

Drehidtarsna, in Limerick: cross bridge.

Dressoge (also **Dressogagh**), a briery or bushy place.

Dresternagh (also **Dresternan**, **Dristernan**), *see* Dressoge.

Drim, a form of *druim*, a ridge.

Drimeen (also **Drimmeen**), little ridge.

Drimna (also **Drimnagh**), ridges, a place full of ridges or hills.

Drinagh (also **Drinaghan**), a place producing *dreens* or blackthorns.

Drinan (also **Drinaun**), *see* Dreenan.

Drishaghaun (also **Drishane**, **Drishoge**), *see* Dressoge.

Droghed, *Droichead*, a bridge.

Drogheda, *Droichead-atha* (Drohedaha), F.M., the bridge of the ford, from the ford across the Boyne used before the erection of a bridge.

Drom, *Druim*, a ridge or long hill.

Dromada (also **Dromadda**), long *druim* or ridge.

Drombeg (also **Drumbeg**), small ridge.

Dromcolliher, in Limerick: a corruption of *Druim-Collchoille* (Drum-Collohill), the ridge of the hazel wood.

Dromdaleague, in Cork: the ridge of the two *liags* or pillar stones.

Dromgarriff, rough ridge.

Dromin, *see* Drom.

Dromineer, in Tipperary: *Druim-inbhir* (Druminver), the ridge of the *inver* or river mouth, because it is situated near where the Nenagh river enters Lough Derg.

Dromkeen, beautiful ridge.

Dromore, great ridge or long hill.

Dromtrasna, cross ridge.

Drum, *Druim*, a ridge or long hill.

Drumad, *Druim-fhada*, long ridge.

Drumadoon, the ridge of the *dun* or fort.

Drumahaire, in Leitrim: *Druim-da-ethiar* (Drum-a-ehir), F.M. the ridge of the two air-demons.

Drumanure, the ridge of the yew tree.

Drumany (also **Drummany**), ridges, ridged land.

Drumard, high ridge or long hill.

Drumatemple, the ridge of the temple or church.

Drumavaddy, the ridge of the dog (*madadh*).

Drumballyroney, the ridge of O'Roney's town.

Drumbane (also **Drumbaun**), white ridge.

Drumbarnet, the ridge of the gap (*bearna*).

Drumbo (also **Drumboe**), *Druimbo*, F.M., the cow's ridge.

Drumbrughas, the ridge of the farmhouse.

Drumcanon, the ridge of the white-faced cow: *ceann-fhionn* (canon), whitehead.

Drumcar, in Louth: *Druim-caradh* (Drumcara), F.M., the ridge of the weir.

Drumcliff, in Sligo: *Druim-chliabh* (Drumcloev), F.M., the ridge of the baskets.

Drumcolumb, St Columba's ridge.

Drumcondra, Conra's ridge.

Drumcrin, the ridge of the tree (*crann*).

Drumcrow, the ridge of the cattle sheds (*cro*).

Drumcullen (also **Drumcullion**), the ridge of holly.

Drumderg, *Druim-dearg*, red ridge.

Drumduff, *Druim-dubh*, black ridge.

Drumfad, *Druim-fada*, long ridge.

Drumgill, the ridge of the *Gall* or foreigner.

Drumgoose (also **Drumgose**) the ridge of the calves (*cuas*).

Drumgowna (also **Drumgownagh**), *Druim-gamhnach*, the ridge of the heifers.

Drumharrif (Drumherriff), *Druim-thairbh* (Drum-har-riv), the ridge of the bull.

Drumhillagh *see* page 8.

Drumhirk, *druim-thuirc*, the ridge of the boar.

Drumhome, in Donegal. In O'C. Cal. the name is written *Druim-Thuama* (Drumhooma), and Adamnan translates it *Dorsum Tommae*, the ridge of Tomma, a pagan woman's name.

Drumillard (also **Drummillar**), the eagle's ridge (*iolar*).

Drumkeen, beautiful ridge.

Drumkeeran, the ridge of the quicken trees.

Drumlane, *Druim-leathan* (lahan), F.M. broad ridge.

Drumlease, *Druim-lias*, the ridge of the huts.

Drumlish, the ridge of the *lis* or fort.

Drumlougher, the ridge of the rushes (*luachra*).

Drumman, *see* Drum.

Drummeen, little ridge.

Drummin, *see* Drum.

Drummond, a corrupt form of Drumman. *See* page 10.

Drummuck, the ridge of the pigs (*muc*).

Drummully, the ridge of the summit (*mullach*).

Drumnacross, the ridge of the cross.

Drumneen, little ridge.

Drumquin, *Druim-Chuinn*, Conn's ridge.

Drumraine (also **Drumrainy**), ferny ridge (*ráthain*).

Drumreagh, *Druim-riabbach*, grey ridge.

Drumroe, *Druim-ruadh*, red ridge.

Drumroosk, the ridge of the *roosk* or marsh.

Drumshallon, the ridge of the gallows (*sealan*).

Drumshanbo, the ridge of the old *both* or tent (*sean*, old).

Drumsillagh, *see* page 8.

Drumsna (also **Drumsnauv**), *Druim-snamha* (snawa), the ridge of the swimming. *See* Lixnaw.

Drumsurn, the ridge of the furnace or kiln (*sorn*).

Duagh, in Kerry: *Dubh-ath* (Dooah), black ford, from a ford on the river Feale.

Dublin The name is written in the annals *Duibh-linn* (Duvlin) which in some of the Latin Lives of the saints is translated *Nigra therma*, black pool. It was originally the name of that part of the Liffey on which the city is built and is sufficiently descriptive at the present day. In very early ages an artificial ford of hurdles was constructed across the Liffey where the main road from Tara to Wicklow crossed the river; and the city that subsequently sprung up around it was called from this circumstance *Ath-cliath* (Ah-clee), F.M., the ford of hurdles which was the ancient name of Dublin. This name is still used by speakers of Irish in every part of Ireland but they join it to Bally – *Baile-atha-cliath* (which they pronounce *Blaa-clee*), the town of the hurdle ford.

Dufferin, barony of, in Down: *Dubh-thrian* (Duv-reen), F.M., the black *treen* or third part.

Duhallow, in Cork: *Duthaigh-Ealla* (Doohy-alla) F.M. The district of the Allo, from the Blackwater river, a portion of which was anciently called the Allo.

Dulane, in Meath: *Tuilen*, F.M., little *tulach* or hill.

Duleek, in Meath: *Daimhliag* (Davleeg), O'C., Cal., stone house or church (*daimh*, a house and *liag*).

Dunamase, in Laois: should have been called Dunmask for the Irish name is *Dun-Masg*, F.M., the fortress of *Masg*, who was one of the ancestors of the Leinster people.

Dunamon, in Galway: so called from a castle of the same name on the Suck; but the name which the annalists write *Dun-Iomgain*, Imgan's fort, was anciently applied to a *dun*, which is still partly preserved.

Dunboe, in Derry: the fortress of the cow.

Dunboyne, *Dun-Baeithin*, *Baeithin's* or Boyne's fort.

Duncannon, Conan's fortress.

Duncormick, Cormac's fortress.

Dundalk The name was originally applied to the great fortress now called the moat of Castletown, a mile inland, which was the residence of *Cuchullin*, chief of the Red Branch Knights in the first century. *Dun-Dealgan* (Dalgan), F.M., the fortress of *Delga*, a Firbolg chief who built it.

Dunderrow, in Cork: written *Dun-dermaigi* (Dundarwah) in the Book of Leinster, the fortress of the oak-plain (*See* Durrow); and the large dun from which it received the name is still in existence, half a mile south of the village.

Dundonald, in Down, Donall's fortress: so called from a fort that stands not far from the church.

Dundrum, *Dun-droma*, F.M., the fortress on the ridge or hill.

Duneane, in Antrim: written in the Felire of Aengus, *Dun-da-én* (Dun-a-ain), the fortress of the two birds.

Dunfanaghy, *Dun-Fionnchon* (Finahan), *Finchu's* fort.

Dungannon, in Tyrone: *Dun-Geanainn* (Gannin), F.M., *Geanan's* or Gannon's fortress.

Dungarvan, *Dun-Garbhain*, F.M., Garvan's fortress.

Dunhill, *Dun-aille*, the fortress of the cliff.

Dunkineely, in Donegal: *Dun-mhic-Chionnfhaelaidh* (Dunvickaneely), Mackineely's fort.

Dunkit, *Ceat's* or Keth's fortress.

Dunleer, in Louth. Old name *Land-léri* (Book of Leinster), the church (*land* or *lann*) of austerity. Present name formed by substituting *dun* a fort for *lann*.

Dunluce castle, near the Giant's Causeway: *Dunlios*. F.M., strong *lios* or fort. *Dun* is here an adjective, meaning strong.

Dunmanway, in Cork. Old name *Dun-na-mbeann* (Dunaman), F.M., the fortress of the gables or pinnacles. The last syllable *way* is from *buidhe* yellow (bwee or with the *b* aspirated wee): Dunmanway, the fortress of the yellow pinnacles.

Dunmore, great fort.

Dunmurry, *Dun-Muireadhaigh*, Murray's fort.

Dunquin, in Kerry: *Dun-caein* (Dunkeen), F.M., beautiful fort.

Dunshaughlin, in Meath. A church was founded here for bishop *Sechnall* or Secundinus, St Patrick's nephew; and hence it was called *Domhnach-Seachnaill* (Donna-Shaughnill), F.M., the church of St *Sechnall*, which has been shortened to the present name.

Duntryleague, in Limerick. According to a passage in the Book of Lismore, a *dun* or place was built here for Cormac Cas, son of Olioll Olum (*see* Connello); and his bed was supported by three *liagáns* or pillar stones, from which the place was called *Dun-tri-liag*, the fortress of the three *liags* or pillar stones.

Durrow, in Offaly, a favourite residence of St Columbkille. Venerable Bede has a short passage in his Eccl. Hist. (lib. iii., cap. iv.), in which the original form and translation of this name are given:

"Before he [Columba] passed over into Britain, he had built a noble monastery in Ireland, which, from the great number of oaks, is in the Scotic [Irish] language called *Dearmhagh* (Darwah), the field of the oaks" (*dair* and *magh*).

Dysart (also **Dysert**), *see* Desert.

Dysartenos, in Laois. St Aengus the Culdee, who died in the year 824, built a cell for himself here and hence the place was called *Disert-Aenghusa*, Aengus's hermitage.

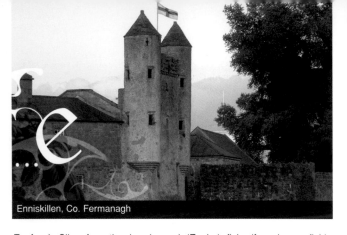

Enniskillen, Co. Fermanagh

Easky, in Sligo: from the river *Iascach* (Eeska), fishy (from *iasg*, a fish).

Eden, *Eudan* (edan), the brow; a hill brow.

Edenderry, the hill brow of the oak wood.

Edenmore, great hill brow.

Edergole (also **Edergoole**), *see* Addergoole.

Eglish, a church: *see* Aglish.

Eighter, *Iochtar* (eeter), lower.

Eliogarty, in Tipperary: a shortened form of Ely O'Fogarty (shortened by having the *f* aspirated and omitted: *see* page 8), O'Fogarty's *Ely*, so called from its ancient possessors the O'Fogartys. *See* Ely.

Elphin, in Roscommon. St Patrick founded a church here near a spring over which stood a large stone; and hence the place was called *Aill-finn*, which Colgan interprets the rock (*aill*) of the clear spring (*finn* white, clear).

Ely The different tribes called *Eile* or *Ely* were so named from their ancestor *Eile*, the seventh in descent from *Cian*, son of Olioll Olum (*see* Connello).

Emlagh, *Imleach* (Imlagh), land bordering on a lake; and hence a marshy or swampy place.

Emly, in Tipperary: St *Ailbhe* founded his establishment here in the fifth century on the margin of a lake which has only lately drained. The place is called in the Irish authorities *Imleach-iobhair* (yure), the lake-marsh of the yew tree.

Emlygrennan, in Limerick: a corruption of the Irish name *Bile-Ghroidhnín* (Billa-Gryneen), Grynan's ancient tree.

Enagh, the name of twenty townlands. Sometimes *Aenach*, a fair, sometimes *Eanach*, a marsh.

Ennereilly, in Wicklow: *Inbher-Daeile* (Invereela), F.M., the *inver* or mouth of the river formerly called the Deel, now the Pennycomequick.

Ennis, *inis*, an island: a meadow along a river.

Enniskeen, *Inis-caein* (keen), F.M., beautiful island or river meadow.

Enniskerry, *Ath-na-scairbhe* (Annascarvy), the ford of the *scarriff* or rough river crossing, from an ancient stony ford where the old road crosses the river.

Enniskillen, *Inis-Cethlenn* (Kehlen), F.M., the island of *Kethlenn*, wife of Balor, the Fomorian king of Tory Island.

Ennistimon, *Inis-Diomain*, F.M., *Diaman's* river meadow.

Errigal, *Aireagal*, a habitation, a small church.

Errigal Keeroge, in Tyrone: *Aireagal Dachiarog* (Dakeeroge), F.M., the church of St *Dachiarog*.

Errigal Trough, in Monaghan: the church of (the barony of) Trough.

Esker, *Eiscir*, a sandhill.

Eskeragh (also **Eskragh**), a place full of *eskers*.

Ess (also **Essan**, **Essaun**), a waterfall.

Estersnow, in Roscommon: a strange corruption from the Irish *Disert-Nuadhan* (Nooan), F.M., the hermitage of St *Nuadha* (Nooa). Disert is often corrupted to *ister*, *ester*, *tirs*, *tristle*, etc.

Near Fivemiletown, Co. Tyrone

Faddan, *Feadan*, a small brook.

Faha (also **Fahy**), an exercise green. *See Faithche* in Irish Root Words.

Farnagh (also **Farnane**, **Farnoge**), a place of *fearns* (farns), or alders.

Farney, in Monaghan: *Fearnmhagh* (Farnvah), Book of R., the alder plain (*fearn* and *magh*).

Farran, *fearann*, land.

Farset (also **Farsid**), *fearsad*, a sandbank in a river.

Fartagh (also **Fertagh**), a place of graves (*feart*).

Fasagh (also **Fassagh**), a wilderness (*fásach*).

Fassadinin, in Kilkenny: the *fasagh* or wilderness of, or near, the river Dinin.

Feagh, *Fiodhach* (Feeagh), a woody place (*fidh*).

Fearmore, great grass (*féur*) or grassy place.

Feddan, *see* Faddan.

Feenagh, *Fiodhnach* (Feenagh), woody (*fidh*); a woody place.

Feighcullen, in Kildare: *Fiodh-Chuilinn*, F.M., Cullen's wood.

Fenagh, *see* Feenagh.

Fennor, *Fionnabhair* (Finner), F.M., white field.

Fermanagh, so called from the tribe of *Fir-monach*, O'Dugan, the men of *Monach*, who were originally a Leinster tribe, so named from their ancestor, *Monach*, fifth in descent from Cahirmore, monarch of Ireland from AD120 to 123.

Fermoy, in Cork: *Feara-muighe* (Farra-moy), O'Dugan, the men of the plain.

Fermoyle, *Formaeil*, a round hill.

Fernagh (also **Ferney**), *see* Farnagh.

Ferns, *Fearna* (Farna), F.M., alders, a place abounding in alders: English plural termination added.

Ferrard, barony of, in Louth: *Feara-arda* (Farra-arda), F.M., the men of the height, i.e. of Slieve Bregh.

Fethard, *Fiodh-ard* (Fecard), F.M., high wood.

Fews, baronies of, in Armagh: *Feadha* (Fa), F.M., woods; with the English plural termination added. Fews in Waterford has the same origin.

Fiddan, (also **Fiddane**, **Fiddaun**), *see* Faddan.

Fiddown, in Kilkenny: *Fidh-duin* (Feedoon), F.M., the wood of the *dun* or fort.

Fingall, a district lying north of Dublin in which the Danes settled and hence it was called *Fine-Gall* (O'C. Cal.), the territory or tribe (*fine*) of the *Galls* or foreigners.

Finglas, clear stream (*fionn*, white, clear; and *glaise*, small river).

Finn river and lake in Donegal: *Loch-Finne*, the lake of *Finna*, a woman about whom there is an interesting legend. The river took its name from the lake. *See* Origin and History of Irish Names of Places.

Finnea, in Westmeath: *Fidh-an-atha* (Fee-an-aha), F.M., the wood of the ford.

Fintona, *Fionn-tamhnach* (Fintowna), F.M., fair coloured field.

Fivemiletown, Tyrone, named for its relative isolation from other towns. An Irish mile until 1826 was about 1¼ times the length of an English mile.

Foil, *Faill*, a cliff.

Foilduff, black cliff.

Forenaght (also **Forenaghts**, **Fornaght**, **Farnaght**), *Fornocht*, a bare, naked or exposed hill.

Formil (also **Formoyle**, **Formweel**), *see* Fermoyle.

Forth The descendants of Ohy Finn *Fothart* (Fohart), brother of Conn of the Hundred Battles (king of Ireland from AD 123 to 158) were called *Fotharta* (Foharta), Book of R. Some of them settled in the present counties of Wexford and Carlow, where the two baronies of Forth still retain their name.

Foy (Foygh), forms of *Faithche*. *See* Faha.

Foybeg (also **Foymore**), little and great exercise green.

Foyduff, black exercise green.

Foyle, *see* Foil.

Freagh (also **Freugh**), *Fraech*, heath, a heathy place.

Freagduff (also **Freeduff**), black heath.

Freaghillan (also **Freaghillaun**), heathy island (*oileán*).

Freshford, Irish name *Achadh-úr* (Book of Leinster), which should have been translated Freshfield: *Achadh* was mistaken for *ath*.

Freughmore (also **Freaghmore**), great heath.

Funcheon, *Fuinnseann* (Funshin), the ash tree: the ash-producing river.

Funshin (also **Funshinagh**, **Funshog**, **Funshoge**), a place producing ash trees (*fuinnse*).

Giant's Causeway, Co. Antrim

Galbally (also **Gallavally**, **Galvally**, **Galwally**), English town; *Gall* here means an Englishman.

Galboley (also **Galboola**, **Galbooley**, **Galwolie**), a *booley* or dairy place belonging to *Galls* or English people.

Gallagh, a place full of rocks or standing stones. See *Gall* in Irish Root Words.

Gallan (also **Gallane**), *Gallan*, a standing stone.

Gallen The descendants of *Cormac Gaileng*, great grandson of Olioll Olum (*see* Connello) were called *Gailenga* (O'Dugan), the race of Gaileng, and they gave name to the barony of Gallen in Mayo.

Gallon is used in Cavan to signify a measure of land.

Gallow, *see* Gallagh.

Gardrum (also **Gargrim**), *Gearr-dhruim*, short ridge or hill: *d* changed to *g* in Gargrim (*see* page 10).

Garnavilla, in Tipperary: *Garran-a'-bhile* (Garranavilla), the shrubbery of the *bile* or old tree.

Garracloon, *Garbh-chluain*, rough meadow.

Garran (also **Garranbaun**), white shrubbery.

Garranekinnefeake, Kinnefeake's shrubbery.

Garry, a garden (*garradha*).

Garryard, high garden.

Garrycastle The Mac Coghlans' castle, near Banagher in Offaly, is

71

called in the annals *Garrdha-an-chaislein* (Garrancashlane), the garden of the castle; and from this the modern name Garrycastle has been formed and extended to the barony.

Garryduff, black garden (*dubh*).

Garrymore, great garden.

Garryowen, near Limerick: Owen's garden.

Garrysallagh, dirty garden (*salach*).

Garryspellane, Spellane's garden.

Gartan, a little garden. See *Gort* in Irish Root Words.

Garvagh, *Garbhach*, rough land (from *garbh*, rough).

Garvaghy, rough *achadh* or field.

Garvary, *Garbhaire*, rough land.

Gay island in Fermanagh, goose island (*gedh*).

Geara (also **Gearagh**, **Gairha**), *Gaertha* (gairha) a bushy place along a river.

Gearhameen river, at Killarney: *min* smooth, small; *gearha* composed of small delicate bushes.

Giant's Causeway The Irish name for the area is *Clochán-na-bhFomharaigh* (Clohanavowry), the *cloghan* or stepping stones of the Fomorians. These sea rovers were magnified into giants in popular legend, and the name came to be translated 'Giant's Causeway'.

Girley, in Meath: *Greallach* (Grallagh), a miry place.

Glack, *Glaic*, a hollow.

Glanbehy, birchy glen (*beith*).

Glantane (also **Glantaun**), little glen.

Glanworth, in Cork: recently corrupted from its Irish name *Gleann-amhnach* (Glenounagh) as it is written in the Book of Rights, the watery or marshy glen.

Glascloon, green *cloon* or meadow.

Glasdrummon (also **Glasdrummond**), green ridge.

Glashaboy (also **Glashawee**), yellow streamlet (*glaise* and *buidhe*).

Glasheen, a little stream.

Glasmullagh, green *mullach* or summit.

Glasnevin, near Dublin: takes name from a streamlet flowing through Delville into the Tolka at the bridge. In remote ages some pagan chief named *Naeidhe* (Nee) must have resided on its banks; from him it was called *Glas-Naeidhen* (Neean), F.M., *Naeidhe's* streamlet; and the name extended to the village while its original application is quite forgotten.

Glassan, a green place.

Glasthule, *Glas-Tuathail* (thoohil), *Tuatha's* or Toole's streamlet.

Glenagarey, *Gleann-na-gcaerach* (Glenagaira), the glen of the sheep (*caera*).

Glenanair, the glen of slaughter (*ár*).

Glenavy, in Antrim. The *G* is a modern addition. The Irish name as given in the Calendar is *Lann-Abhaich* (Lanavy), the church of the dwarf. When St Patrick had built the church there he left it in charge of his disciple Daniel who, from his low stature, was called *Abhac* (avak or ouk), i.e. dwarf.

Glenbane (also **Glenbaun**), white glen.

Glencar, on the borders of Leitrim and Sligo: *Gleann-a'-chairthe* (Glenacarha), the glen of the pillar stone (*cairthe*).

Glencullen (also **Glencullin**), holly glen (*cuillion*).

Glendine (also **Glandine**), deep glen (*doimhin*).

Glendowan mountains, in Donegal: *see* Glendine.

Glenduff, black glen (*dubh*).

Glengarriff, rough or rugged glen (*garbh*).

Gleninagh, ivy glen (see *Eidhneán* in Irish Root Words).

Glenkeen, beautiful glen.

Glenmore, great glen.

Glennamaddy, the valley of the dogs (*madadh*).

Glenogra, in Limerick: Ogra's glen.

Glenosheen, in Limerick: *Oisin's* or Osheen's glen.

Glenquin, barony of, in Limerick: *see* page 9.

Glenreagh (also **Glenrevagh**), grey glen.

Glenroe, red glen (*ruadh*).

Glentane (also **Glentaun**), little glen.

Glenties, in Donegal: *Gleanntaidhe* (glenty), glens: from two fine glens at the head of which it stands.

Glenwhirry, in Antrim: *Gleann-a'-choire* (glenacurry: change of *ch* to *wh*), the glen of the river Curry or *Coire*. *Coire* means a cauldron, and the river got this name from a deep pool formed under a cataract.

Glynn, a glen or valley.

Gneeve (also **Gneeves**), *Gniomh* (gneeve), a measure of land.

Gola, forks, the plural of *gabhal* (goul).

Golan, a little *goul* or fork.

Golden, in Tipperary: *Gabhailin* (Gouleen), a little fork: the Suir divides there for a short distance forming a fork.

Gort, *Gort*, a tilled filled.

Gortahork (also **Gortahurk**), the field of the oats (*coirce*).

Gortalassa, the field of the *lis* or fort.

Gortanure (also **Gortinure**), the field of the yew.

Gortavoher, the field of the *boher* or road.

Gortboy, yellow field (*buidhe*).

Gortbrack, speckled field (*breac*).

Gorteen, little field.

Gortfad (also **Gortfadda**), long field.

Gortgranagh, grain field.

Gortin, little field: *see* Gorteen.

Gortmore, great field.

Gortnaglogh, *Gort-na-gclogh*, the field of the stones.

Gortnagross, *Gort-na-gcros*, the field of the crosses.

Gortnahoo (also **Gortnahoon**), the field of the cave (*uaimh*).

Gortnamona, the field of the bog (*moin*).

Gortnamucklagh, the field of the piggeries. *See* Mucklagh.

Gortnasillagh, the field of the sallows.

Gortnaskea (also **Gortnaskeagh**, **Gortnaskeha**, **Gortnaskey**), the field of the *sceachs* or whitethorn bushes.

Gortreagh, grey field (*riabhach*).

Gortroe, red field (*ruadh*).

Gougane Barra, in Cork: St Finbar's rock-cleft.

Goul (also **Gowel**), *Gabhal*, a fork.

Gowlan (also **Gowlane**, **Gowlaun**), little fork.

Graffa (also **Graffin**, **Graffoge**, **Graffy**), grubbed land, or land rooted up by a *grafaun* or grubbing axe.

Graigue, a village.

Graiguenamanagh, the village of the monks.

Grallagh, *Greallach* (Grallagh), a miry place.

Granagh (also **Granaghan**), a place producing grain.

Grangegeeth, windy grange (*gaeth*).

Gransha, a grange, a place for grain.

Greagh, a moory level spot among hills.

Great Connell, great *congbhail* or habitation (*see* Conwal).

Greenan (also **Greenane**, **Greenaun**, **Grenan**), *Grianan*, a summer residence, a royal palace. From *grian*, the sun.

Greenoge, a sunny little spot. From *grian*.

Grillagh (also **Grellagh**), *see* Grallagh.

Gurteen, little tilled field; *see* Gorteen.

Gurteenroe, red little field.

Guilcagh, a place producing broom (*giolcach*, broom).

Gyleen, near Trabolgan in Cork: little *gobhal* or fork.

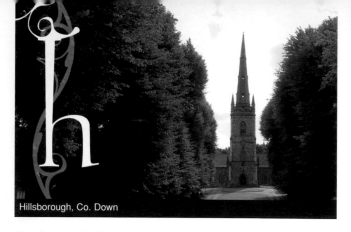
Hillsborough, Co. Down

Heagles, near Ballymoney: *Eaglais*, a church.

Hillsborough, Down, named after the English army officer Moyses Hill, 17th century landowner, but originally known in Irish as Cromghlinn, or 'crooked valley'.

Howth, from the Danish *Hoved*, a head. Old Irish name *Ben Edar*, the peak of Edar, a legendary personage.

Innisfree, on Lough Gill, Co. Leitrim

Idrone, baronies of, in Carlow. So called from the tribe of *Hy Drona* (Book of R.), the former occupants who were named from their ancestor *Drona*, fourth in descent from Cahirmore, monarch of Ireland from AD 120 to 123.

Illan (also **Illane**, **Illaun**), *Oileán* (oilaun), an island.

Imaile, in Wicklow: *Hy Mail* (O'Dugan), the descendants of Mann *Mal*, brother of Cahirmore. *See* Idrone.

Inch, *Inis*, an island; a low meadow along a river.

Inchmore, great island or river meadow.

Inish (also **Inish**), an island.

Inishannon, in Cork: written in the Book of Leinster *Inis-Eoganain* (Inishowenan), Owenan's or little Owen's island or river meadow.

Inishargy, in Down: called in the Taxation of 1306, *Inys-cargi*, showing that the Irish form is *Inis-carraige*, the island of the rock. The rising ground where the church stands was formerly surrounded by marshes.

Inishbofin, the island of the white cow (*bo*), name explained by a legend.

Inishkeen, beautiful island.

Inishkeeragh, the island of sheep (*caera*).

Inishlounaght, in Tipperary: *Inis-leamhnachta* (lounaghta), the island or river holm of the new milk, probably because it was good grazing land.

Inishmaan (also **Inishmean**), middle island (*meadhon*).

Inishmacsaint, a parish in Fermanagh, taking its name from an island in Lough Erne, which is called in the annals *Inis-muighe-samh* (moy-sauv), the island of the plain of sorrel, from which the present name has been formed by a corrupt pronunciation.

Inishmore, great island.

Inishowen, in Donegal: the island of Owen, son of Niall of the Nine Hostages (king from 379 to 405). *See* Tyrone.

Inishrush, the island of the peninsula (*ros*).

Inishturk, in Mayo: *Inis-tuirc*, Hy F., the boar's island (*torc*). Several islands of this name.

Inishtioge, in Kilkenny: written in the Book of Leinster *Inis-Teoc*, *Teoc's* island.

Innisfallen, in the lower Lake of Killarney: called in the Book of Leinster *Inis-Faithlenn* (Fahlen), the island of *Faithlenn*, a man's name.

Innisfree Innis or *inis* meaning island, and free from the Gaelic *fraoch* for heather. The famous 'lake isle' of Yeats' poem lies in Lough Gill.

Inver, *Inbhear* (inver), the mouth of a river.

Ireland's Eye Original name *Inis-Ereann* (Eran) (the island of *Eire* or Eria, a woman), of which the present name is an attempted translation. *Eye* is the Danish *ey*, an island, and the translators understanding *Ereann* to mean Ireland, rendered the name Ireland's *Ey* (or island) instead of Eria's *Ey*. (*See* Origin and History of Irish Names of Places, pp. 76, 101, 104.)

Isertkelly, in Galway: corrupted (similarly to the next two names) from *Diseart-Cheallaigh* (Disertkelly), F.M., *Cellach's* or Kelly's hermitage.

Isertkieran, in Tipperary: the *desert* or hermitage of St Kieran of Ossory. *See* Seirkieran.

Ishartmon, in Wexford: the *desert* or hermitage of St Munna. *See* Taghmon.

Island Magee, the island or peninsula of the *Mac Aedhas* or Magees, its former possessors. Anciently called *Rinn-Seimhne* (Rinn-sevne), the point of *Seimhne*, the old territory in which it was situated.

Iverleary, in Cork: took its name from the O'Leary, its ancient proprietors. *See* Iverk.

Iverk, in Kilkenny: *Ui-Eirc* (Ee-erc), O'Dugan, a tribe name, signifying the descendants of *Erc*. *Ui* (ee) or *uibh* (iv), signifies descendants.

Iveruss, in Limerick: the old tribe of *Uibh-Rosa* the descendants of *Rosa*.

Kenmare, Co. Kerry

Kanturk, in Cork: *Ceann-tuirc* (Kanturk), F.M., the boar's head or hill; from the hill near the town.

Keadew (also **Keady**), *Ceide* (Keady), a hill level and smooth at top.

Keale (also **Keel**), *Caol*, narrow; a narrow place, valley, or river.

Keeloge (also **Keeloges**), *Caelóg*, a narrow stripe or ridge

Keelty, *Coillte* (Coiltha), woods, from *coill*.

Keenagh (also **Keenaghan**), a mossy place (*caenach*, moss).

Keenaght barony in Londonderry. The descendants of *Cian* (Kean), son of Olioll Olum (*see* Connello) were called *Cianachta* (Keenaghta), i.e. the race of *Cian*. The O'Conors of Glengiven, who were a portion of this tribe, possessed the barony of Keenaght and gave it its name.

Keimaneigh, pass of, in Cork: *Ceim-an-fhiaigh* (Kame-an-ee), the pass of the deer (*fiadh*).

Kenmare, *Ceann-mara*, the head of the sea (*muir*), i.e. the highest point reached by the tide in a river. *See* Kinvarra and Kinsale.

Kerry The descendants of *Ciar* (Keer: *see* Connemara) were called *Ciarraidhe* (Keery: Book of R.), i.e. the race of *Ciar*. They possessed the territory lying west of Abbeyfeale which was called from them *Ciarraighe*, and ultimately gave name to the whole county.

Kesh, in Fermanagh: *Ceis* (Kesh), a wickerwork causeway.

Keshcarrigan, in Leitrim: the wickerwork causeway of the little rock.

Kilbaha, *Coill-beithe*, birch wood.

Kilbarron, in Donegal; St Barron's church.

Kilbarry, in Waterford and Cork: from St Finbar. *See* Cork and Gougane Barra.

Kilbeg, small church or wood.

Kilbeggan, Beccan's church.

Kilbeheny, *Coill-beithne*, (Kilbehena), F.M., birch wood.

Kilbreedy, *Cill-Bhrighde*, St Brigid's church.

Kilbride, *see* Kilbreedy.

Kilbroney, church of *Bronagh*, a virgin saint.

Kilcarragh, in Kerry and Waterford: the church of St *Carthach* (Caurha) of Lismore.

Kilcavan, in Wexford: church dedicated to St Kevin of Glendalough.

Kilcleagh (also **Kilclay**), *see* Kilclief.

Kilclief, in Down: *Cill-cleithe* (Kilcleha), the hurdle church (*cliath*). The original church was constructed of hurdles after the early Irish fashion.

Kilcolman, St Colman's church.

Kilcommon, St Colman's church.

Kilcullen, *Cill-cuillinn*, the church of the holly.

Kildalkey, in Meath: written in an Irish charter in the Book of Kells, *Cill-Delga*, Delga's church.

Kildare According to Animosus, St Brigid built her little cell here under a very high oak tree and hence it was called *Cill-dara*, which the same writer translates *Cella quercûs*, the cell or church of the oak.

Kildimo, in Limerick: St Dima's church.

Kildorrery, in Cork: *Cill-diarbhre* (Kildarrery), the church of the oaks. *See* Darraragh.

Kildrought, in Kildare. *See* Celbridge.

Kilduff, black church or wood.

Kilfinnane, in Limerick: the church of St Finan. *See* Ardfinnan.

Kilfithmone, in Tipperary: the church of the wood of the bog (*fidh* and *móin*).

Kilflyn, Flann's church.

Kilgarriff (also **Kilgarve**), rough wood.

Kilgarvan, *St Garbhan's* or Garvan's church.

Kilkee, in Clare: St *Caeidhe's* (Kee's) church.

Kilkeedy, in Clare and Limerick: St *Caeide's* (Keedy's) church.

Kilkeel, narrow church.

Kilkenny, *Cill-Chainnigh*, F.M., the church of St *Cainneach* or Canice who died in the year 598. *See* Aghaboe.

Killadysart, the church of the *desert* or hermitage.

Killaloe, in Clare and Kilkenny: *Cill-Dhalua* (Klllaloo, *d* aspirated, *see* page 7), the church of St Dalua or Molua who flourished in the sixth century.

Killanummery, in Leitrim: *Cill-an-iomaire* (ummera), F.M., the church of the ridge.

Killarney, *Cill-airne*, the church of the sloes.

Killashandra The original church was built within the enclosure of a rath or fort which still partly exists, hence *Cill-a'-sean-ratha* (Killashanraha), the church of the old rath.

Killashee, in Kildare: *Cill-ausaille*, the church of St *Ausaille* or Auxilius, a contemporary of St Patrick. Killashee in Longford is probably the church of the *sidh* or fairy hill.

Killaspugbrone, near Sligo. In the Book of Armagh it is stated that St Patrick built a church at *Cassel Irra* for his disciple *Brón* or Bronus who became bishop of *Cuil Irra*, the peninsula lying south-west of Sligo: hence the place was called *Cill-easpuig-Bróin*, F.M., the church of bishop Bronus (*easpug*, a bishop).

Killaspuglonane, in Clare: *Cill-easpuig-Fhlannáin*, F.M., the church of bishop Flannan.

Killawillin, in Cork: *Cill-a'-mhuilinn*, the church of the mill.

Killeany, in Clare and Galway: the church of St Eany or Endeus of Aran who flourished in the fifth century.

Killeedy, in Limerick: the church of the virgin saint Ita or *Ide* who founded a nunnery here in the early part of the sixth century. *See* Kilmeedy.

Killeen, the name of more than 80 townlands, nearly all from *Cillín* a little church, but a few from *Coillín*, a little wood.

Killeentierna, in Kerry, *Tighernach's* (Tierna's) little church.

Killeigh, in Ofaly: *Cill-achaidh* (Killahy), F.M., the church of the field.

Killenaule, in Tipperary: the church of St *Naile* (Nawly) or Natalis.

Killery harbour, in Connemara: corrupted by a change of *l* to *r* (*see* page 9), from *Cael-shaile* (Keelhaly), narrow sea-inlet, but the full name is *Cael-shaile-ruadh*, F.M., the reddish (*ruadh*) narrow sea-inlet.

Killevy (also **Killeavy**), in Armagh: called from its proximity to Slieve Gullion, *Cill-shleibhe* (Killeva), F.M., the church of the *sliabh* or mountain.

Killiney, in Dublin: corrupted from *Cill-inghen* (Kilineen); full name *Cill-inghen-Leinín*, the church of the daughters of *Leinin*.

Killiney, in Kerry: *see* Killeany.

Killisk (also **Killiskey**), the church of the water (*uisge*).

Killoe, *Cill-eó*, O'C. Cal., the church of the yews.

Killure, *Cill-uibhair*, the church of the yew.

Killursa, *Cill-Fhursa*, the church of St Fursa who flourished in the sixth century.

Killybegs, *Cealla-beaga*, F.M., little churches.

Killygorden, in Donegal: *Coill-na-gcuiridin* (Kilnagurridin), F.M., the wood of the parsnips.

Killyon, the church of St *Liadhan* (Leean) or Liedania, mother of St *Ciaran* of Ossory. *See* Seirkieran.

Kilmacanoge, in Wicklow: the church of St *Mochonog*, one of the primitive Irish saints.

Kilmacrenan, in Donegal: *see* page 9.

Kilmainham, near Dublin: *see* page 9.

Kilmallock, in Limerick: *Cill-Mocheallog* (Kilmohelog), the church of St *Mocheallog*, who flourished in the beginning of the seventh century.

Kilmanagh, near Kilkenny: *Cill-manach* (Mart. Taml.), the church of the monks.

Kilmeedy, the church of St *Mide* or Ité, for both are the same name. *See* Killeedy.

Kilmihil, the church of St Michael the Archangel.

Kilmore, there are about 80 parishes and townlands of this name, most of them signifying great church, some great wood (*cill* and *coill*).

Kilmurry There are more than fifty places of this name, which were all so called from places dedicated to the Blessed Virgin: *Cill-Mhuire*, Mary's church.

Kilnaleck, the wood of the flag-surfaced land.

Kilnamanagh, in Tipperary: *Coill-na-manach*, F.M., the wood of the monks.

Kilnamona, the church of the bog (*moin*).

Kilpatrick, St Patrick's church.

Kilquane, *Cill-Chuain*, St Cuan's church.

Kilrook, in Antrim: *Cill-ruadh*, F.M., red church.

Kilrush, the church of the wood or peninsula.

Kilskeer, in Meath: the church of the virgin saint *Scire*, who flourished in the sixth century.

Kiltenanlea, in Clare: *Cill-tSeanin-leith*, the church of St Senan the hoary.

Kiltullagh, in Roscommon: *Cill-tulaigh*, the church of the hill.

Kiltybegs, *Coillte-beaga*, little woods.

Kilwatermoy, in Waterford: *water* is here a corruption of *uachtar*, upper: the church of the upper plain.

Kinalea, barony of, in Cork: *Cinel-Aedha* (Kinel-Ay), O'Dugan, the descendants of *Aedh* or Hugh who was the father of *Failbhe-Flann*, king of Munster in AD 636.

Kinalmeaky, barony of, in Cork: *Cinel-mBece* (Kinelmecka), O'Dugan, the descendants of *Bece*, the ancestor of the O'Mahonys.

Kinard, *Ceann-ard*, high head or hill.

Kinawley, in Fermanagh: *Cill-Naile* (Kilnawly, which would have been the correct anglicised form), O'C. Cal., the church of St *Naile* or Natalis who died in AD 564.

Kincon, the hound's head (*ceann* and *cu*).

Kincora, at Killaloe, the site of Brian Boru's palace, took its name from an ancient weir across the Shannon: *Ceann-coradh* (Kancora), F.M., the head or hill of the weir.

Kinneigh (also **Kinnea**), *Ceann-ech*, F.M., the horse's head or hill.

Kinnitty, in Offaly: *Ceann-Eitigh* (Kan-Etty), *Etech's* head. So called, according to a gloss in the Felire of Aengus, because the head of *Etech*, an ancient Irish princess, was buried there.

Kinsale (also **Kinsaley**), *Ceann-saile*, the head of the brine, i.e. the highest point to which the tide rises in a river. See Kenmare.

Kinure, *Ceann-uibhair*, the head of the yew.

Kinvarra, in Galway: *Ceann-mhara*, F.M., the head of the sea. See Kenmare.

Knappagh, *Cnapach*, a place full of *cnaps* or round hillocks.

Knock, *Cnoc*, a hill.

Knockacullen, the hill of the holly.

Knockaderry, the hill of the oak wood.

Knockagh, *Cnocach*, a hilly place.

Knockainy, in Limerick: the hill of *Aine* or Ainy, a celebrated *banshee*.

Knockalisheen, the hill of the little *lis* or fort.

Knockalough, the hill of the lake.

Knockane (also **Knockaun**), little hill.

Knockanglass (also **Knockaneglass**), green little hill.

Knockanree, *see page 8.*

Knockanroe (Knockaneroe, Knockaunroe), red little hill.

Knockanure, *Cnoc-aniubhair*, yew hill.

Knockatemple, the hill of the temple or church.

Knockatirriv (also **Knockatarry**, **Knockaterriff**), *Cnoc-a'-tairbh*, the hill of the bull.

Knockatober, the hill of the well.

Knockatoor, the hill of the *tuar* or bleach green.

Knockatotaun, *Cnoc-a'-teotain*, the hill of the burning or conflagration.

Knockaunbaun, white little hill.

Knockavilla (also **Knockaville**), the hill of the *bile* or old tree.

Knockavoe near Strabane: *Cnock-Buidhbh* (Knockboov), F.M., the hill of Bove Derg, a legendary Tuatha De Danann chief.

Knockbane (also **Knockbaun**), white hill.

Knockboy, *Cnoc-buidhe*, yellow hill.

Knockbrack, *Cnoc-breac*, speckled hill.

Knockcroghery, in Roscommon: the hill of the *crochaire* or hangman. It was a place of execution.

Knockdoo (also **Knockduff**), *see page 7.*

Knockeen, little hill.

Knockfierna, in Limerick: *Cnoc-fírinne*, the hill of truth, or of truthful prediction, for it serves as a weather glass to the people of the circumjacent plains who can predict whether the day will be wet or dry by the appearance of the summit in the morning.

Knockglass, *Cnoc-glas*, green hill.

Knockgorm, *Cnoc-gorm*, blue hill.

Knocklayd, in Antrim: called from its shape *Cnoc-leithid* (lehid), the hill of breadth, i.e. broad hill.

Knocklofty, in Tipperary: *Cnoc-locht*, the *lofted* or shelving hill.

Knocklong, in Limerick: *cnoc-luinge*, the hill of the encampment for

Cormac mac Art encamped with his army on this hill when he invaded Munster in the third century.

Knockmanagh, middle hill.

Knockmealdown mountains, *Cnoc-Maeldomhnaigh*, Maeldowney's hill.

Knockmore, great hill.

Knockmoyle, *Cnoc-mael*, bald or bare hill.

Knockmullin, the hill of the mill.

Knocknaboley (also **Knocknabooly**), the hill of the *booley* or dairy place.

Knocknacrohy, *Cnoc-na-croiche*, the hill of the gallows; a place of execution.

Knocknagapple (also **Knocknagappul**), *Cnoc na-gcapall*, the hill of the horses.

Knocknagaul, in Limerick: the hill of the *Galls* or foreigners.

Knocknageeha, the hill of the wind (*gaeth*).

Knocknagin, *Cnoc-na-gceann* (na-gan), the hill of the heads; a place of execution.

Knocknaglogh, the hill of the stones (*cloch*).

Knocknagore, the hill of the goats (*gabhar*).

Knocknahorna, the hill of the barley (*eórna*).

Knocknamona, the hill of the bog.

Knocknamuck, the hill of the pigs.

Knocknarea, in Sligo: the hill of the executions. *See* Ardnarea.

Knocknaskagh (also **Knocknaskeagh**), the hill of the *sceachs* or white thorn bushes.

Knockninny, a hill in Fermanagh, which gives name to a barony, *Cnoc-Ninnidh* (ninny), the hill of St *Ninnidh*, who was a contemporary of St Columba.

Knockpatrick, Patrick's hill.

Knockraha (also **Knockrath**, **Knocknaraha**), the hill of the *rath* or fort.

Knockranny, *Cnoc-raithnigh* (rahnee), ferny hill.

Knockrawer (also **Knockramer**, **Knockrower**, **Knockrour**), *Cnoc-reamhar* (rawer or rower), *fat* or thick hill.

Knockreagh, grey hill.

Knockroe, red hill.

Knockshanbally, the hill of the old town.

Knocksouna, near Kilmallock in Limerick: written in the Book of Lismore *Cnoc-Samhna* (Souna), the hill of *Samhain* (Sowan or Savin), the first of November, which was kept as a festival by the pagan Irish. *See* Origin and History of Irish Names of Places, page 194.

Knocktemple, the hill of the temple or church.

Knocktopher, in Kilkenny: *see* pages 9-10.

Knoppoge (also **Knappoge**), a little hill. *See* Knappagh.

Kyle, about half the names partly or wholly formed from Kyle are from *Cill*, a church; the other half from *Coill*, a wood.

Kylebeg, small church or wood.

Kylemore, generally great wood (*coill*), sometimes great church (*cill*). Kylemore (lake) near the Twelve Pins in Connemara is *Coill-mhor*, great wood.

Red roof near Kiltyclogher, Co. Leitrim

Labba (also **Labby**), *Leaba* (labba), a bed, a grave.

Labbasheeda, in Clare: *Leaba-Sioda*, *Sioda's* or Sheedy's *labba*, bed or grave.

Labbamolaga, St Molaga's grave. *See* Templemolaga.

Lack, *leac* (lack), a stone, a flagstone.

Lacka, the side of a hill.

Lackabane (also **Lackabaun**), white hill side.

Lackagh, a place full of stones or flags.

Lackamore, great hill side.

Lackan, *see* Lacka.

Lackandarragh (also **Lackendarragh**), the hillside of the oaks.

Lackareagh, grey hill side (*riabhach*).

Lackaroe, red hill side (*ruadh*).

Lackeen, a little rock or flag.

Lacken, *see* Lacka.

Lag (also **Legg**), a hollow; a hollow in a hill.

Lagan, a little hollow. Sometimes it means a pillar stone (*liagan*). The river Lagan probably took its name from a little hollow on some part of its course.

Laghil (also **Laghile**), *Leamhchoill* (Lavwhill), elm wood.

Laght, *Leacht*, a sepulchre or monument.

Laghy, a slough, a miry place.

Laharan, *Leagh-fhearann* (Laharan), half land.

Lahard, *Leath-ard*, half height; a gentle hill.

Lahardan (also **Lahardane**, **Lahardaun**), a gentle hill.

Lakyle, *Leath-choill*, half wood.

Lambay island near Dublin. The latter part is Danish: Lame-ey, i.e. lamb island. Its ancient Irish name was *Rechru* or *Reachra*; and the adjacent parish on the mainland was called from it, *Port-Reachrann* (Portrahern), the port or landing place of *Reachra*, which in the course of ages has been softened down to the present name, Portraine.

Laragh (also Lauragh), *Lathrach*, the site of any thing.

Laraghbryan, in Kildare: Bryan's house site.

Largan, *Leargan*, the side or slope of a hill.

Largy, *Leargaidh*, *see* Largan.

Larne, in Antrim: *Latharna* (Laharna: Book of L.), the district of *Lathair* (Laher), son of Hugony the Great, monarch of Ireland before the Christian era. Until recently it was the name of a district which extended northwards towards Glenarm and the town was then called *Inver-an-Laharna*, the river mouth of (the territory of) Larne, from its situation at the mouth of the *Ollarbha* or Larne Water.

Latt, *see* Laght.

Latteragh, in Tipperary: *Leatracha* (Latraha), the plural of *Leitir*, a wet hillside (*see* Letter). It is called in O'C. Cal., *Letracha-Odhrain* (Oran), *Odhran's* wet hill-slopes, from the patron St *Odhran* who died in the year 548.

Laughil, *Leamhchoill* (Lavwhill); elm wood.

Laune river, at Killarney: *Leamhain*, F.M., elm; the elm-producing river.

Lavagh, *Leamhach* (Lavagh), a place producing elms.

Lavally, *Leath-bhaile*, half town or townland.

Lavey, in Cavan: *see* Lavagh.

Leagh, *Liath* (Leea), grey; a grey place.

Leam, *Leim*, a leap.

Leamlara, in Cork, the mare's leap.

Leamnamoyle, in Fermanagh: the leap of the *mael* or hornless cow.

Lear, *see* Lyre.

Lecale, barony of, in Down, *Leth-Chathail* (Lecahil), F.M., *Cathal's* half. *Cathal* was a chief who flourished about the year 700 and in a division of territory this district was assigned to him and took his name.

Lecarrow, *Leth-ceathramhadh* (Lecarhoo), half quarter (of land).

Leck, *see* Lack.

Leckan (also **Leckaun**), *see* Lacka.

Leckpatrick, Patrick's flagstone.

Leeg (also **Leek**, **Leeke**), *see* Lack.

Legacurry (also **Legaghory**), *Lag-a-choire* (curry), the hollow (*lag*) of the caldron or pit.

Legan (also **Legaun**), *see* Lagan.

Legland, *see* Leighlin. *D* added: *see* page 10.

Lehinch, *Leith-innse*, F.M., half island, i.e. a peninsula.

Leighlin, in Carlow: *Leith-ghlionn* (Leh-lin), F.M., half glen; from some peculiarity of formation in the little river bed.

Leighmoney, grey *muine* or shrubbery.

Leinster In the third century before the Christian era, *Labhradh Loingseach* (Lavra Linshagh, Lavra the mariner) brought an army of Gauls from France to assist him in recovering the kingdom from his uncle, the usurper, Coffagh Cael Bra. These foreign soldiers used a kind of broad pointed spear called *laighen* (layen) and from this circumstance the province in which they settled, which had previously borne the name of *Galian*, was afterwards called *Laighen* which is its present Irish name. The termination *ster*, which has been added to the names of three of the provinces, is the Scandinavian or Danish *stadr*, a place. *Laighenster* (the place or province of *Laighen*) would be pronounced *Laynster*, which is the very name given in a state paper of 1515 and which naturally settled into the present form, Leinster.

Leitrim, the name of more than 40 townlands and villages: *Laith-dhruim* (Lee-drum), F.M., grey *druim* or ridge.

Leixlip, a Danish name meaning salmon leap (*lax*, a salmon), from the well-known cataract on the Liffey, still called Salmon leap, a little above the village. By Irish-Latin writers it is often called *Saltus-salmonis* (the leap of the salmon), and from this word *saltus*, a leap, the baronies of Salt in Kildare have taken their name.

Lemanaghan, in Offaly: *Liath-Manchain*, F.M., St Manchan's grey land.

Lena (also **Leny**), a wet meadow.

Lenamore, great wet meadow.

Lerrig, in Kerry: a hill side. *See* Largan.

Letter, *Leitir*, a wet hill side.

Lettera (also **Letteragh**, **Lettery**), wet hill-sides. *See* Latteragh.

Letterkenny, a shortened form of *Letter-Cannanan*, the O'Cannanans' hill-slope. The O'Cannanans, or as they now call themselves, Cannons, were anciently chiefs or kings of Tirconnell until they ultimately sank under the power of the O'Donnells.

Lettermacaward, in Donegal: *Leitir-Mic-a'-bhaird*, the hill slope of Mac Ward, or the bard's son.

Lettermore, great wet hill-side.

Lettermullan, *Leitir-Meallain*, F.M., Meallan's hill-slope.

Levally, *see* Lavally.

Levny The descendants of *Luigh* or Lewy, the son of *Cormac Gaileng* (*see* Gallen), were called *Luighne* (Leyny: O'Dugan), and they gave name to the barony of Leyny in Sligo (*ne*, descendants).

Lick, *see* Lack.

Lickbla, in Westmeath: shortened from *Liag-Bladhma* (Leeg-Blawma), F.M., the flag-stone of *Bladh* (Blaw), a man's name. *See* Slieve Bloom.

Lickeen, little flag-stone.

Lickfinn, in Tipperary: white flag-stone.

Lickmolassy, in Galway: St *Molaise's* (Molasha's) flag-stone.

Lickoran, the flag of the cold spring (*uaran*).

Limerick, corrupted from the Irish form Liumnech (*Liminagh*), F.M., by a change of *n* to *r* (*see* page 9): the name signifies a bare spot of land, from *lom*, bare.

Lis (also **Liss**), *Lios*, a circular earthen fort.

Lisalbanagh, the *Albanagh's* or Scotsman's fort.

Lisanisk (also **Lisanisky**), the fort of the water (*uisge*).

Lisbane (also **Lisbaun**), white *lis* or fort.

Lisbellaw, *Lios-bel-atha*, the *lis* of the ford-mouth.

Lisboy, yellow fort; probably from furze blossoms.

Liscannor, in Clare: Canar's fort.

Liscarrol, in Cork: *Cearbhall's* or Carroll's fort.

Liscartan, the fort of the forge (*ceardcha*).

Lisdoonvarna, in Clare: takes its name from a large fort on the right of the road as you go from Ballyvaghan to Ennistymon. The proper name of this is *Dunbhearnach* (Doonvarna) gapped fort (*see* Barna), from its shape, and the word *Lis* was added, somewhat in the same manner as 'river' in the expression 'the river Liffey': Lisdoonvarna, i.e. the *lis* (of) Doonvarna.

Lisdowney, in Kilkenny: Downey's fort.

Lisduff (also **Lisdoo**), *Lios-dubh*, black fort.

Lisheen, little *lis* or fort.

Lislea, *Lios-liath* (lee), grey fort.

Lislevane, in Cork: *Lios-leamhain*, elm fort.

Lismore, great fort. Lismore in Waterford received its name from the *lis* or entrenchment built by St *Carthach* (Caurhagh) round his religious establishment. It was previously called *Magh-sciath* (Maskee), the plain of the shield. *See* Origin and History of Irish Names of Places, page 261.

Lismoyle, *Lios-mael*, bald or dilapidated fort.

Lismullin, the fort of the mill.

Lisnagat, *Lios-na-gcat*, the fort of the (wild) cats.

Lisnageeragh, the fort of the sheep (*caera*).

Lisnalee, the fort of the calves (*laegh*). *See* pages 9-10.

Lisnamuck, the *lis* or fort of the pigs.

Lisnaskea, in Fermanagh: the fort of the *sceach* or white-thorn tree. It took its name from the celebrated *Sceach-ghabhra* (Skagowra), under which the Maguire used to be inaugurated.

Lisnisk (also **Lisnisky**), the fort of the water.

Lissan (also **Lissane**), little *lis* or fort.

Lissaniska (also **Lissanisky**), the fort of the water.

Lissaphuca, the fort of the *pooka* or sprite.

Lissard, high fort.

Listowel, *Lios-Tuathail* (Lis-Thoohil), *Tuatha's* fort.

Lissonuffy, in Roscommon: *Lios-O-nDubhthaigh* (Lisonuffy), F.M., the fort of the O'Duffys.

Lixnaw, in Kerry: *Lic-Snamha* (snawa), F.M., the flag-stone of the swimming (*snamh*). *See* Drumsna.

Loughill (also **Loughil**), *Leamhchoill* (Lavwhill), elm wood.

Londonderry Its most ancient name, according to all our authorities, was *Doire-Chalgaich* (Derry-Calgagh), the derry or oak wood of *Calgach* or *Galgacus*. In the tenth or eleventh century it began to be called *Derry-*

Columcille in honour of St Columbkille who founded his monastery there in 546, and this name continued to the time of James I whose charter, granted to a company of London merchants, imposed the name of Londonderry.

Longfield, in almost all cases a corruption of *Leamh-choill* (Lavwhill), elm wood.

Longford, *Longphort* (Longfort), a fortress. The town of Longford is called in the Annals Longford O'Farrell, from a castle of the O'Farrells, the ancient proprietors.

Loop Head, in Clare: a Danish modification of Leap Head; Irish *Leim-Chonchuillinn* (Leam-Conhullin), F.M., *Cuchullin's* leap. For legend *see* Origin and History of Irish Names of Places, page 163.

Lorum, in Carlow: *Leamh-dhruim* (Lavrum), elm ridge.

Lough, a lake; an inlet of the sea.

Loughan (also **Loughane**, **Loughaun**), little lake.

Loughanreagh, grey little lake.

Loughbeg, little lake.

Lough Boderg, the lake of the red cow.

Lough Bofin, the lake of the white cow.

Loughbrickland, corrupted by changing *r* to *l*, and adding *d* (*see* page 10) from *Loch-Bricrenn*, F.M., the lake of *Bricriu*, a chief of the first century.

Lough Conn, in Mayo: *Loch-Con*, F.M., the lake of the hound.

Lough Corrib, the correct Irish name is *Loch Orbsen*, F.M., which was corrupted by the attraction of the *c* sound in *Loch* to *Orbsen*, and by the omission of the syllable *sen*. *Orbsen* was another name for *Manannan Mac Lir*, a celebrated legendary personage.

Loughcrew, in Meath: *Loch-craeibhe* (creeve), the lake of the branchy tree.

Lough Derg, on the Shannon: contracted from *Loch-Dergdherc* (Dergerk), the lake of the red eye, which is explained by a legend.

Lough Derravara, in Westmeath: *Loch-Dairbhreach* (Darravara), F.M., the lake of the oaks. *See* Darraragh.

Lough Erne, the lake of the *Ernai*, a tribe of people.

Lough Finn, *see* Finn river.

Lough Guitane, near Killarney: *Loch-coiteáin* (cut-thaun), the lake of the little *cot* or boat.

Lough Melvin, corrupted from *Loch-Meilghe* (Melye), the lake of *Meilghe*, an ancient king of Ireland.

Lough Neagh, written in the Book of Leinster *Loch nEchach* (nehagh), the lake of *Eochy* (Ohy), a Munster chief who was drowned in it at the time of its eruption in the first century. The *n* is a mere grammatical inflection and the name is often used without it; for instance, we find it spelled *Lough Eaugh* in Camden, as well as in many of the maps of the 16th and 17th centuries.

Lough Oughter, in Cavan: *Loch-uachtar*, upper lake, i.e. upper as regards Lough Erne.

Loughrea, in Galway: *Loch-riabhach*, grey lake.

Lug, a hollow: *see* Lag.

Lugduff mountain, over Glendalough: black hollow, from a hollow at the base.

Luggelaw, the hollow of the *lagh* or hill.

Lugmore, great hollow.

Lugnaquillia, the highest mountain in Wicklow: *Lug-na-gcoilleach* (Lugnagulllagh), the hollow of the cocks, i.e. grouse.

Lumcloon, bare meadow (*lom*, bare).

Lurgan, the shin; a long hill.

Lurganboy, yellow long hill.

Lurraga, *see* Lurgan.

Lusk, in Dublin: *Lusca*, a cave.

Lusmagh, in Offaly: the plain of herbs (*lus*, a herb).

Lynally In the sixth century there was a forest here called the wood of Ela and the church founded by St Colman about the year 590 was thence called *Lann-Ealla* (O'C. Cal.), the church of *Ela*, which has been anglicised to the present name.

Lynn, a form of *Lann*, a house or church.

Lyre, *Ladhar* (Lyre), a fork formed by rivers or glens. *See* Lear.

Outside Tomney's Pub, The Moy, Co. Tyrone

Mace, *Más* (Mauce), the thigh, a long low hill.

Mackan (also **Mackanagh**, **Macknagh**, **Mackney**), a place producing parsnips (*meacan*, a parsnip).

Macosquin, in Derry: corrupted from *Magh-Cosgrain* (Macosgran), F.M., *Cosgran's* plain.

Maghera, *Machaire*, a plain. Maghera in Down and Maghera in Derry are both contracted from *Machaire-ratha* (Maghera-raha), the plain of the fort.

Magherabeg, little plain.

Magheraboy, yellow plain.

Magheracloone, the plain of the *cloon* or meadow.

Magheraculmoney, the plain of the back (*cul*) of the shrubbery.

Magheradrool, in Down: *Machaire-eadarghabhal* (Maghera-addrool), the plain between the (river) forks (*eader*, between and *gabhal*). See Addergoole.

Magherahamlet, in Down: the plain of the *Tamlaght* or plague monument. *See* Tallaght.

Magheramenagh, middle plain (*meadhonach*).

Magheramore, great plain.

Magherareagh, grey plain (*riabhach*).

Maghery, a form of Maghera, a plain.

Magunihy, barony of, in Kerry: *Magh-gCoincinne* (Magunkinny), F.M., the plain of the O'Conkins.

Mahee island, in Strangford Lough: the island of St *Mochaei* (Mohee), bishop, a disciple of St Patrick, and the founder of Nendrum.

Maigue, a river in Limerick: called *Maigh* in the annals, i.e. the river of the plain.

Mallow, in Cork: called in the Annals *Magh-Ealla* (Moyalla), the plain of the river Allo which was anciently the name of that part of the Blackwater flowing by the town. *See* Duhallow.

Manulla, in Mayo: *Magh-Fhionnalbha* (Mah-Innalva), Hy. F., Finalvan's plain.

Massereene, in Antrim: *Más-a'-rioghna* (Massareena), the queen's hill.

Maul, *Meall*, a lump, a hillock.

Maum, *Madhm* (Maum), a high mountain pass.

Maumturk, the pass of the boars (*torc*).

Maw, *Magh*, a plain.

Maynooth, *Magh-Nuadhat* (Ma-nooat), F.M., *Nuadhat's* plain, from *Nuadhat*, king of Leinster, foster-father to Owen More king of Munster. *See* Bear.

Mayo, *Magh-eó* (Ma-ó), the plain of the yews. Full name *Magheó-na-Saxan*, F.M., Mayo of the Saxons, from a number of English monks settled there in the seventh century by St Colman, an Irish monk, after he had retired from the *see* of Lindisfarne.

Meelick, *Miliuc* (Meeluck), F.M., low marshy ground.

Meen, a mountain meadow.

Meenadreen, the mountain meadow of blackthorns.

Meenkeeragh, mountain meadow of the sheep.

Milleen, a little hillock. *See* Maul.

Moan, *Móin* (mone), a bog.

Moanduff, black bog.

Moanmore, great bog.

Moanroe, red bog.

Moanvane (also **Moanvaun**), *Móin-bhán*, white bog.

Moat, *Móta*, a high mound.

Moate, in Westmeath: from the great mound at the village; full name Moategranoge, the moat of *Graine-óg* or young Grace, who, according to tradition, was a Munster princess.

Mocollop, the plain (*magh*) of the *collops* or cattle.

Modeshill, *Magh-deisiol* (Ma-deshil), southern plain.

Mogeely, *Magh-Ile*, F.M., the plain of *Ile* or Ely.

Moher, *see* Cliffs of Moher.

Mohill, *Maethail* (Mwayhill), soft or spongy land; from *maeth*, soft.

Moig (also **Moigh**), forms of *Magh*, a plain.

Moira, *Magh-rath*, F.M., the plain of the forts.

Mon, *see* Moan.

Monabraher (also **Monambraher**, **Monamraher**), *Moin-na-mbrathar*, F.M., the bog of the friars.

Monagay, in Limerick: the bog of the goose (*gedh*); from wild geese.

Monaghan, *Muineachois*, F.M., a place full of little hills or brakes (*muine*)

Monamintra, in Waterford: *Mois-na-mbaintreabhaigh* (Monamointree), the bog of the widows.

Monard, high bog.

Monasteranenagh, in Limerick: *Mainister-an-aenaigh* (Monasteraneany), F.M., the monastery of the fair. In ancient times it was called *Aenach-beag*, little fair.

Monasterboice, in Louth: the monastery of St *Boethius* or *Buite*, who founded it in the sixth century.

Monasterevin, the monastery of St Evin, the founder a contemporary of St Patrick.

Monasteroris, in Offaly: *Mainister-Fheorais*, (orish: *F* aspirated and omitted: *see* page 8), the monastery of Mac *Feorais* or Bermingham, who founded it in AD 1325.

Monear, a meadow.

Moneen, a little bog (*moin*).

Money, *Muine* (munny), a shrubbery.

Moneydorragh, *Muine-dorcha*, dark or gloomy shrubbery.

Moneyduff, *Muine-dubh*, black shrubbery.

Moneygall, the shrubbery of the *Galls* or foreigners.

Moneygorm, *Muine-gorm*, blue shrubbery.

Moneymore, great shrubbery.

Monivea, in Galway: *Muine-an-mheadha* (Money-an-va), F.M., the shrubbery of the mead, a kind of drink.

Monroe, *Moin-ruadh*, red bog.

Montiagh (also **Montiaghs**), *Mointeach*, a boggy place.

Morgallion A branch of the *Gailenga* (*see* Gallen), settled in Leinster, and a portion of them gave name to the territory of *Mor-Gailenga* or the great *Gailenga*, now the barony of Morgallion in Meath.

Mothel (also **Mothell**), *see* Mohill.

Mountmellick The old anglicised name is *Montiagh-meelick*, the bogs or boggy land of the *meelick* or marsh. *See* Montiagh and Meelick.

Mourne mountains, in Down. The ancient name was *Beanna Boirche* (Banna-Borka), F.M., the peaks of the shepherd *Boirche*, who herded on these mountains the cattle of *Ross*, king of Ulster in the third century. About the middle of the twelfth century, a tribe of the MacMahons from Cremorne (*see* Cremorne) settled in the south of the present county of Down and gave their tribe name of *Mughdhorna* (Mourna), to the barony of Mourne, and to the Mourne mountains.

Movilla, in Down: *Magh-bhile* (Ma-villa), O'C. Cal., the plain of the ancient tree.

Moville, in Donegal: *see* Movilla.

Moy, *Magh* (mah), a plain.

Moyacomb, in Wicklow: *Magh-da-chon* (Moy-a-con), F.M., the plain of the two hounds.

Moyaliff, in Tipperary: *Magh-Ailbhe* (Moyalva), F.M., *Ailbhe's* or Alva's plain.

Moyard, high plain.

Moyarget, *Magh-airgid*, the plain of silver.

Moyarta, in Clare: *Magh-fherta* (*fh* silent: *see* page 8), the plain of the grave.

Moycullen, in Galway, the plain of holly.

Moydow, in Longford: *Magh-dumha* (Moy-dooa), F.M., the plain of the burial mound.

Moygawnagh, in Mayo: written in the Book of Lecan, *Magh-gamhnach*, the plain of the milch cows.

Moyglass, green plain.

Moygoish The descendants of *Colla Uais* (*see* Cremorne) were called *Ui mic Uais* (Ee-mic-Oosh), a portion of whom were settled in Westmeath and gave their name to the barony of Moygoish.

Moyle, *Mael*, a bald or bare hill.

Moylough, the plain of the lake.

Moymore, great plain.

Moynalty, in Meath: *Magh-nealta* (Moynalta), the plain of the flocks (*ealta*).

Moyne, *Maighin* (Moin), a little plain.

Moynoe, in Clare: same as Mayo; the *n* is a grammatical accident.

Moynure, the plain of the yew (*iubhar*).

Moyrus, the plain of the *ros* or peninsula.

Moys, i.e. plains; from *magh*.

Muckamore, in Antrim: *Magh-comair* (Ma-cummer), F.M., the plain of the *cummer* or confluence (of the Six Mile Water with Lough Neagh).

Muckanagh (also **Muckenagh**), *Muiceannach*, a resort of pigs; a place where pigs used to feed or sleep (from *muc*).

Muckelty (also **Mucker**, **Muckera**, **Muckery**),*see* Muckanagh.

Mucklagh, *Muclach*, *see* Muckanagh.

Muckinish, pig island.

Muckloon (Mucklone, Mucklin), *Muc-chluain*, pig meadow.

Muckno, in Monaghan: *Mucshnamh* (Mucknauv), F.M., the swimming place (*snamh*) of the pigs; the place where pigs used to swim across the little lake.

Muckross, the peninsula of the pigs.

Muff, a corruption of *Magh*, a plain.

Muing, a sedgy place.

Mullacrew, in Lough: *Mullach-craeibhe* (Mullacreeva), the summit of the spreading tree.

Mullagh, *Mullach*, a summit.

Mullaghareirk mountains, near Abbeyfeale in Limerick: *Mullach-a'-radhairc* (rirk), the summit of the prospect.

Mullaghbane, white summit.

Mullaghboy, yellow summit.

Mullaghbrack, speckled summit.

Mullaghdoo (also **Mullaghduff**), black summit.

Mullaghglass, green summit.

Mullaghmeen, *Mullach-mín*, smooth summit.

Mullaghmore, great summit.

Mullaghroe, *Mullach-ruadh*, red summit.

Mullan (also **Mullaun**), a little *mullach* or summit.

Mullans, little summits.

Mullen (also **Mullin**), *Muileann* (mullen), a mill.

Mullinahone, in Tipperary: *Muileann-na-huamhainn* (Mullinahooan), the mill of the cave (*uamha*); from a cave near the village through which the little river runs.

Mullinavat, in Kilkenny: *Muilenn-a'-bhata*, the mill of the stick.

Mully, *see* Mullagh.

Multyfarnham, in Westmeath: *Muilte-Farannain* (Multy-Farannan), Farannan's mills (*muilenn*, plural *muille*).

Munster Old Irish name *Mumhan* (Mooan), which with *ster* added (*see* Leinster), forms *Mughan-ster* (Moonster) or Munster.

Murragh (also Murreagh), *Murbhach* (Murvagh), a flat marshy piece of land by the sea.

Murrow of Wicklow: *see* Murragh.

Muskerry The people descended from Carbery Musc, son of Conary II (*see* Corkaguiny) were called *Muscraidhe* (Muskery: O'Dugan). Of these there were several tribes, one of which gave name to the two baronies of Muskerry in Cork.

Myshall, in Carlow: *Muigh-íscal* (Mweeshal), low plain.

Bridge over the River Strule, Newtownstewart, Co. Tyrone

Naas, in Kildare, the most ancient residence of the kings of Leinster, *Nás* (Nawce), a fair or meeting place.

Nantinan, in Limerick: *Neantanán*, a place of nettles (*neanta*).

Nappan, in Antrim, *Cnapán*, a little hill.

Naul, in the north of Dublin, *'n-aill* (naul), the cliff. The article incorporated: *see* Nenagh.

Ned, *Nead* (Nad), a bird's nest.

Nenagh, in Tipperary. Irish name *Aenach* (Enagh), a fair; the *N* is a contraction for the Irish definite article 'an' which has become incorporated with the word: *'n-Aenach* (Nenagh), the fair. The full name is *Aenach-Urmhumlan* (Enagh-urooan), the fair of Ormond or east Munster and this name is still used by those speaking Irish.

Newrath, *'n-Iubhrach* (Nuragh), the yew land; by the incorporation of the article.

New Ross Irish name *Ros-mic-Treoin* (Rosmictrone), the wood (*ros*) of the son of *Treon*.

Newry Ancient name *Iubhar-cinn-tragha* (Yure-Kintraw), the yew tree at the head of the strand. In after ages this was shortened to *Iubhar* which, with the article prefixed (*see* Nenagh), and *y* added, became changed to the present form Newry.

Newtownstewart Sir William Stewart gave his name to the area during the Plantation, granted by King Charles I. The area was once a stronghold of the powerful O'Neill family; the ruins of Harry Avery O'Neill's 14th century castle lie near the town.

Nicker, in Limerick: *Cuinicér* (Knickere), a rabbit warren (from *coiní*).

Nobber, *Obair* (obber), work, with the article incorporated (*see* Nenagh): Nobber, 'the work', a name applied according to tradition to the English castle erected there.

Nohoyal, in Cork and Kerry: shortened from *Nuachongbhail* (Nuhongval), new *congbhail* or habitation. *See* Conwal.

Nure, *see* Newry.

Nurney, in Kildare and Carlow: *Urnaidhe* (urny), F.M., a prayer house or oratory, with the article incorporated. *See* Nenagh and Urney.

The Ox Mountains, Co. Sligo

Offaly, baronies of, in Kildare. The descendants of *Ros-failghe* (faly) or *Ros* of the rings, the eldest son of Cahirmore (king of Ireland from AD 120 to 123) were called *Hy Failghe* (O'Dugan), i.e. the descendants of *Failghe* (see Iverk), and a portion of their ancient inheritance still retains this name, in the modernised form Offaly.

Offerlane, in Laois: a tribe name; *Ui Foirchealláin* (Hy Forhellane), F.M., the descendants (*ui*) of *Foircheallán*.

Oghill, *Eóchaill* (Oghill), yew wood (*eó* and *coill*).

Oneilland *Niallán*, the fourth in descent from *Colla Da Chrioch* (cree), brother of Colla Meann (see Cremorne), was the progenitor of the tribe called *Hy Niallain* (ie Niallan's race), F.M., and their ancient patrimony forms the two baronies of Oneilland in Armagh which retain the name. *D* added; see page 10.

Oola, in Limerick and Waterford; *Ubhla* (Oola), a place of apples, an orchard (from *ubhall* or *abhall*).

Oran, *Uaran* (uran), a cold spring.

Oranmore, in Galway: great cold spring.

Oughterard, upper height (*uachdar*, upper).

Oulart, in Wexford: *abhall-ghort* (oulort), an orchard, compounded of *abhall* and *gort*.

Ounageeragh river, flowing into the Funcheon: *Abh-na-gcaerach*, the river of the sheep.

102

Ovens, The near Ballincollig in Cork: called in Irish *Uamhanna* (Oovana), i.e. the caves, from the great limestone caves near the village. The people by a slight change of pronunciation have converted these *oovans* or caves into *ovens*. *See* Athnowen.

Owbeg river, *Abh-beag*, little river.

Owenass river, at Mountmellick: the river of the cataract (*eas*).

Owenboy, yellow river (*abhainn*).

Owenclogy, stony river (*abhainn* and *cloch*).

Owenduff, black river.

Owenmore, Abhainn-mór, *great river*.

Owenreagh, grey river (*riabhach*).

Oxmanstown (also **Ostmantown**), in Dublin: so called because the Danes or Ostmen had fortified settlement there.

Ox mountains: called in Irish *Sliabh-ghamh* (Slievegauv), F.M., the mountains of the storms which in the spoken language was mistaken for *Sliabh-dhamh*, the mountain of the oxen, and translated accordingly.

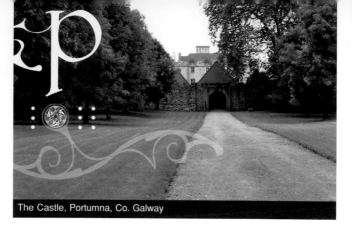

The Castle, Portumna, Co. Galway

Park, Irish *Pairc*, a field.

Parkmore, great field.

Phoenix Park, in Dublin, took its name from a beautiful spring well near the Viceregal Lodge called *Fionn-uisg'* (feenisk), clear or limpid water.

Poll, a hole, pit or pool.

Pollacappul, *Poll-a'-chapaill*, the hole of the horse.

Pollagh, a place full of holes or pits.

Pollanass, at Glendalough: the pool of the waterfall.

Pollans, holes, pools or pits.

Pollaphuca, the *pooka's* or demon's hole.

Pollrone, in Kilkenny: *Poll-Ruadhain* (Ruan), *Ruadh-an's* hole.

Pollsallagh (also **Pollsillagh**), the hole of the sallows.

Portlaw, in Waterford: *Port-lagha*, the bank or landing place of the hill.

Portmarnock, St Mernoc's bank or landing place.

Portnashangan, the *port*, bank or landing place of the *seangans* or pismires [ants].

Portraine, see Lambay island.

Portrush, in Antrim: *Port-ruis*, the landing place of the peninsula.

Portumna, in Galway: *Port-omna*, F.M., the landing place of the oak.

Pottle, in Cavan: a measure of land.

Preban (also **Prebaun**, **Pirbbaun**), *Preabán*, a patch.

Pubble, *Pobul*, people, a congregation.

Pubblebrien, in Limerick: O'Brien's people; for it was the patrimony of the O'Briens.

Pullagh, a place full of holes.

Pullans (also **Pullens**), little holes or pits.

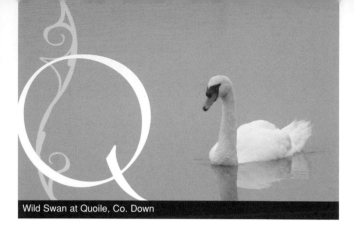
Wild Swan at Quoile, Co. Down

Quilcagh mountain at the source of the Shannon in Cavan, *Cailceach*, chalky; from its white face.

Quilly, *Coillidh* (cuilly), woodland.

Quilty, Clare from *coillte*, a derivation of *coillidh*, woodland. It may also mean 'destroyed', and may refer to earlier maritime tragedies along this stretch of coastline.

Quoile, Down, from the Irish word *coill*, wooded. This place name may also be derived from *caol* or narrow, referring to the River Quoile.

Rossnowlagh Bay, Co. Donegal

Racavan, *Rath-cabhain*, the fort of the hollow.

Rahan, in Offaly: *Raithin*, a ferny place.

Rahaniska (also **Rahanisky**), the rath of the water.

Rahard, *Rath-ard*, high fort.

Raharney, in Westmeath. *Rath-Athairne*, Aharny's fort.

Raheen, little rath or fort.

Raheenduff, black little fort.

Raheenroe, *Raithín-ruadh*, red little fort.

Rahelty, *Rath-eilte*, the fort of the doe (*eilit*).

Raheny, near Dublin: *Rath-Enna*, F.M., Enna's fort.

Rahugh, in Westmeath: the fort of St *Aedh* or Hugh, the son of *Brec*, who built a church in the old rath in the sixth century.

Raigh, *see* Rath.

Rakeeragh, the fort of the sheep (*caera*).

Ramoan, in Antrim: *Rath-Modhain*, Modan's fort.

Ranaghan (also **Rannagh**), a ferny place (*raithne*, a fern).

Raphoe, in Donegal: *Rath-bhoth* (Ra-voh), F.M., the fort of the *boths*, tents or huts.

Rasharkin, in Antrim: *Ros-Earcáin*, Erkan's promontory.

Rashee, in Antrim: *Rath-sithe* (Ra-shee), F.M., the fort of the fairies.

Ratass, in Kerry: *Rath-teas*, southern fort.

Rath, a circular fort.

Rathangan, in Kildare: *Rath-Iomghain* (Rath-Imgan), Imgan's fort.

Rathanny, *Rath-eanaighe*, the fort of the marsh.

Rathaspick, the fort of the bishop (*easpug*).

Rathbane (also **Rathbaun**), white rath.

Rathbeg, little fort.

Rathborney, in Clare: *Rath-boirne*, the fort of Burren, from its situation in the old district of Burren.

Rathcormack, Cormac's fort.

Rathdowney, in Laois: *Rath-tamhnaigh* (Rathtowney), F.M., the fort of the green field (*tamhnach*).

Rathdrum, the fort of the long hill.

Rathduff, black fort.

Rathfeigh, in Meath: the fort of the exercise green. *See* Faha.

Rathfryland, Rathfriland in Down: *see* page 10.

Rathglass, green fort.

Rathkeale, *Rath-Gaela*, Gaela's fort.

Rathkenny, *Rath-Cheannaigh* (Kanny), *Ceannach's* fort.

Rathkieran, in Kilkenny: Kieran's fort; from St Kieran of Ossory. *See* Seirkieran.

Rathmore, great fort.

Rathmoyle, bald or dilapidated fort.

Rathmullan, *Rath-Maelain*, F.M., Maelan's rath.

Rathnew, in Wicklow, *Rath-Naoi*, F.M., Naoi's fort.

Rathreagh, *Rath-riabhach*, grey fort.

Rathroe, red fort.

Rathronan, Ronan's fort.

Rathsallagh, *Rath-salach*, dirty fort.

Rathvilly, in Carlow, *Rath-bile*, F.M., the fort of the old tree.

Rattoo, *Rath-tuaidh* (too), northern fort.

Raw, *Rath*, a fort.

Rea, *Reidh*, a coarse mountain flat.

Reask (also **Reisk, Risk**), *Riasg* (Reesk), a marsh.

Reen, *Rinn*, a point of land.

Reisk, *see* Reask.

Relagh, *Reidhleach* (Relagh), *see* Rea.

Relickmurry, *Reilig*, a graveyard: the church of the Blessed Virgin Mary.

Rin (also **Rine**, **Rinn**), *Rinn*, a point of land.

Ring, *see* Rin.

Ringabella, near the mouth of Cork harbour: the point of the old tree (*bile*).

Ringagonagh, near Dungarvan: *Rinn-U' gCuana* (Ogoona), the point or peninsula of the O'Cooneys.

Ringbane (also **Ringbaun**), white point.

Ringcurran, near Kinsale: the point of the *corrán* or reaping hook; from its shape.

Ringrone, near Kinsale: written in the Annals of Innisfallen, *Rinn-róin*, the point of the seal.

Ringvilla (also **Ringville**), *Rinn-bhile* (villa), the point of the *bile* or ancient tree.

Rinneen, little point of land.

Rinville, in Galway: *Rinn-Mhil* (vil), the point of *Mil*, a Firbolg chieftain.

Risk, *see* Reask.

Roeillaun, *Ruadh-oilean* (Roo-illaun), red island.

Rooaun (also **Rooghan**, **Rooghaun**), reddish land (from *ruadh*, red).

Roosk, *Rusg*, a marsh. *See* Reask.

Roosca (also **Rooskagh**, **Roosky**), *Rusgach*, marshy, a marshy place.

Roscommon, Ros-Comain, F.M., Coman's wood, from St *Coman*, who founded a monastery there in the eighth century.

Roscrea, written in the Book of Leinster, *Ros-cre*, Cre's wood.

Roshin, little *ros* or promontory.

Roskeen, *Ros-caein*, beautiful wood.

Ross, in the south generally means a wood; in the north, a peninsula.

Rossbeg, small wood or promontory.

Rossbegh (also **Rossbehy**), west of Killarney: the peninsula of birches (*beith*).

Ross Carbery, in Cork; the latter part from the barony of Carbery in which it is situated: it was anciently called *Ros-ailithir* (allihir), F.M., the wood of the pilgrims.

Ross Castle, at Killarney: from the little *ros* or peninsula on which it stands.

Rosses, in Donegal: i.e. peninsula.

Rossinver, in Leitrim: *Ros-inbhir*, the peninsula of the river mouth; from a point of land running into the south part of Lough Melvin.

Rossnowlagh, Donegal. *Ros* promontory, *Abhall* (owl): headland of the apples or apple trees.

Rossmore, great wood or peninsula.

Rossorry, near Enniskillen: corrupted from *Ros-airthir* (arher), F.M., the eastern peninsula.

Roughan (also **Ruan**), *see* Rooaun.

Rousky, *see* Roosca and Rooskey.

Route The northern part of Antrim was anciently called *Dalriada* (F.M.), i.e. *Riada's* portion or tribe, from Carbery Riada, son of Conary II (*see* Corkaguiny), and the latter part (*Riada*) of this old name is still preserved in the corrupted form of Route.

Rush, in Dublin: *Ros-eo* (Rush-oï), F.M., the peninsula of the yew trees.

Rusheen, small wood; a growth of underwood.

Russagh, *Ros-each*, F.M., the wood of the horses.

Rusky, *see* Roosca and Roosky.

Sunset at Saul, Co. Down

Saggart, in Dublin: contracted for Tassagard, Irish *Teach-Sacra* (Tassacra), O'C. Cal., the house of St *Sacra*, who flourished in the seventh century.

Saint Mullins, in Carlow: Irish name *Tigh-Moling* (Tee-Molling), O'C. Cal., the house of St *Moling*, a native of Kerry who erected a church there about the middle of the seventh century. See Timolin.

Salt, baronies of, in Kildare: see Leixlip.

Santry, in Dublin: *Sentreibh* (Shantrev; Mart. Taml.), old tribe.

Saul, near Downpatrick: *Sabhall* (Saul), a barn. *Dichu*, the prince of the surrounding district, was St Patrick's first convert in Ireland. The chief made the saint a present of his barn to be used temporarily as a church, and hence the place was called *Sabhall-Patrick*, St Patrick's barn, now shortened to Saul.

Scalp *Scealp* (Scalp), a cleft or chasm.

Scarawalsh, in Wexford: Irish name *Sgairbh-a'-Bhreathnaigh* (Scarriff-a-vranny), Walsh's scarriff or shallow ford (see Ballybrannagh), which, with an obvious alteration, has given name to the barony of Scarawalsh.

Scardan (also **Scardaun**), *Scardan*, a cataract.

Scarriff, *Scairbh* (Scarriv), a rugged shallow ford.

Scart, *Scairt* (Scart), a thicket or cluster.

Scartaglin, in Kerry: the thicket of the glen.

Scarteen, a little thicket or cluster.

Scartlea, in Cork: *Scairt-liath*, grey thicket.

Scarva, another form of Scarriff.

Seagoe, *Suidhe-Gobha* (Seegow), the seat of St *Gobha* (gow) or Gobanus.

Seapatrick, Patrick's seat (*suidhe*).

See, *suidhe* (*see*), a seat or sitting place.

Seefin, *Suidhe-Finn* (Seefin), the seat of Finn Mac Coole.

Seein, in Tyrone: same as Seefin, with *f* aspirated and omitted (*Suidhe-Fhinn*).

Seirkieran, near Parsonstown, St *Ciaran* or Kieran of Ossory, disciple of St Finnian of Clonard, erected a monastery in the sixth century at a place called *Saighir* (Sair) which was the name of a fountain, and after the saint's time it was called *Saighir-Chiarain* (Sairkeeran), now contracted to Seirkieran.

Seltan, a place of sallows.

Seskin, *Sescenn*, a marsh.

Sessia (also **Sessiagh**), *Seiseadh* (shesha), the sixth part.

Shallon, *Sealán*, a hangman's rope, a gallows.

Shan, *Sean* (shan), old.

Shanaclogh, *Seancloch*, old stone castle.

Shanacloon, old *cloon* or meadow.

Shanagarry, old *garry* (*garrdha*) or garden.

Shanagolden, in Limerick: *Seangualann* (Shanagoolan), old shoulder or hill.

Shanakill, old church.

Shanavally (also **Shanbally**), old *bally* or town.

Shanbogh (also **Shanbo**), old *both* or tent.

Shandon, old *dun* or fortress.

Shandrum, old *drum* or ridge.

Shangarry, *see* Shanagarry.

Shankill, old church.

Shanmullagh, old *mullach* or summit.

Shantallow, *Sean-talamh* (Shantalav), old land.

Shanvally, old *bally* or town (*b* aspirated).

Shean (also **Sheean**, **Sheeaun**), *Sidheán* (sheeaun), a fairy hill.

Shee, *sidh* (shee), a fairy, a fairy hill.

Sheeroe, red fairy hill.

Sheetrim, *Sidh-dhruim* (Sheedrim), fairy ridge.

Shelburne, barony, in Wexford: from the tribe of *Siol-Brain* (O'Dugan), the seed or progeny of *Bran*.

Shelmaliere, in Wexford: the descendants of Mallere or *Maelughra* (Meelura).

Sheskin, *Sescenn*, a marsh. *See* Seskin.

Shillelagh, in Wicklow: *Siol-Elaigh* (Sheelealy: O'Dugan), the seed or descendants of *Elach*.

Shinrone, in Offaly: *Suidhe-an-róin* (Sheenrone), F.M., the seat of the *rón*, i.e. literally a seal, but figuratively a hirsute or hairy man.

Shrone, *srón*, a nose, a pointed hill.

Shruel (also **Shrule**). *see* page 9.

Sion, *sidheán* (sheeaun), a fairy mount.

Skagh, *Sceach*, a white thorn bush.

Skahanagh (also **Skehanagh**), a place full of *sceachs* or white thorns.

Skeagh (also **Skea**), *see* Skagh.

Skeheen, a little *sceach* or bush.

Skelgagh, a place of *skolligs* or rocks.

Skellig rocks, off the coast of Kerry: *Sceilig* means a rock.

Skerries (also **Skerry**), *Sceir* (sker), a sea rock; *sceire* (skerry), sea rocks.

Skreen (also **Skrine**), *Scrin* (screen), a shrine.

Sleaty, in Laois: *sleibhte* (Sleaty), F.M., i.e. mountains, the plural of *sliabh:* from the adjacent hills of *Slieve* Margy.

Slee, *Slighe* (slee), a road.

Slemish mountain, in Antrim, on which St Patrick passed his youth herding swine, *Sliabh-Mis*, the mountain of *Mis*, a woman's name.

Sleveen, little *slieve* or mountain.

Slieve, *Sliabh* (sleeve), a mountain.

Slieve Anierin, in Leitrim: *Sliabh-an-iarainn*, the mountain of the iron; from its richness in iron ore.

Slievebane (also **Slievebaun**), white mountain.

Slievebeagh, a range of mountains on the borders of Monaghan, Fermanagh and Tyrone: *Sliabh-Beatha* (Slieve Baha), F.M., the mountain of *Bith*, a legendary hero.

Slieve Bernagh, in the east of Clare: *Sliabh-bearnach*, gapped mountain.

See Lisdoonvarna.

Slievebloom, *Sliabh-Bladhma* (Slieve-Blawma), F.M., the mountain of *Bladh* (Blaw), one of the Milesian heroes.

Slieveboy, yellow mountain.

Slieve Corragh, rugged mountain.

Slieve Donard, the highest of the Mourne mountains. *Domhanghart* (Donart), son of the king of Ulidia, and one of St Patrick's disciples, built a little church on the very summit of this mountain; hence it was called *Sliabh-Domhanghart*, *Donart's* mountain, now anglicised Slieve Donard. Its ancient name was Slieve Slanga, from the bardic hero *Slainge*, the son of Parthalon, who was buried on its summit, where his carn is still to be seen.

Slieve Eelim, a mountain range east of Limerick: *Sliabh-Eibhlinne* (Slieve-Evlinne), Evlin's mountain.

Slieve Fuad, near Newtownhamilton in Armagh: Fuad's mountain; from the Milesian hero Fuad, who was slain there.

Slieve League, in Donegal: *Sliabh-liag*, the mountain of the flag-stones.

Slieve Lougher, east of Castleisland in Kerry: *Sliabh-luachra*, rushy mountain.

Slieve Mish, near Tralee: *see* Slemish.

Slievenagriddle, near Downpatrick: the mountain of the griddle; the *griddle* is a *cromlech* on the hill.

Slievenamon, in Tipperary: *sliabh-na-mban*, the mountain of the women. Full name *Sliabh-na-mban-Feimhinn* (Slievenamon-Fevin), the mountain of the women of *Feimheann*, the ancient territory surrounding it.

Slievenamuck, the mountain of the pigs.

Slievereagh, *Sliabh-riabhach*, grey mountain.

Slieveroe, red mountain.

Slievesnaght, the mountain of the snow (*sneach*).

Sligo, named from the river: *Sligeach* (Sliggagh), F.M., shelly river (*slig*, a shell).

Sliguff, a corruption (*see* page 10) from *Slighe-dhubh* (Slee-duv), a black road.

Slyne Head, in Galway: Irish name *Ceann-leama* (Can-leama), the head of the *lyme* or leap (*leim*), which has been corrupted to the present name by changing *m* to *n*, and prefixing *s*. *See* Stabannon.

Solloghod in Tipperary: *Sulchoid* (sollohed), F.M., sallow wood.

Sonnagh, a mound or rampart.

Sragh (also **Srah**), *srath* (srah), a river holm.

Srahan (also **Srahaun**, **Sraheen**), little river holm.

Sroohill, *see* page 9.

Srough, *Sruth* (sruh), a stream.

Sroughmore, great *sruth* or stream.

Sruffaun, *Sruthán* (Sruhaun), a streamlet (page 9).

Stabannon, corrupted from Tabannon, Bannon's house (*teach*), by prefixing *s*. See Slyne head.

Stakallen, in Meath: *Teach-Collain* (Tacollan), F.M., Collan's house.

Staholmog, in Meath: St *Colmoc's* or *Mocholmoc's* house.

Stamullin, in Meath: *Mealan's* house.

Stang, a measure of land.

Stillorgan, in Dublin: *Tigh-Lorcain* (Teelorcan), *Lorcan's* or Laurence's house or church.

Stonecarthy, in Kilkenny: first syllable a corruption of *stang*: Carthy's *stang* or measure of land.

Stonybatter, in Dublin: stony road: See Ballerstown and Booterstown.

Stook, *Stuaic* (stook), a pointed pinnacle.

Stookan (also **Stookeen**), a little *stook* or pointed rock.

Stradbally, *Stradbhaile* (Sradvally), F.M., street-town; a town of one street.

Stradone (also **Stradowan**), *Srath-doimhin* (Sradowan), deep *srath* or river holm.

Stradreagh, grey street.

Straduff, black river holm.

Straffan, in Kildare: *see* Sruffaun.

Straid (also **Strade**, **Sraud**), *Sráid* (Sraud), a street.

Strancally, near Youghal: *Sron-caillighe* (Srone-cally), the hag's nose or point.

Strangford Lough, in Down: a Danish name; *strong fiord* or bay, from the well-known tidal currents at its entrance. Irish name *Loch Cuan*.

Struell, *see* page 9.

Sylaun, a place of sallows.

Stone wall and Castle, Tubber, Co. Galway

Taghadoe, in Kildare: *Teach-Tuae* (Taghtoo), F.M., the house of St Tua.

Taghboy, yellow house.

Taghmon, in Wexford: written in the Book of Leinster *Teach-Munna* (Taghmunna), the house of St Munna or Fintan, who founded a monastery there and died in AD 634.

Tallaght, in Dublin: *Taimhleacht* (Tavlaght), a plague monument. According to the bardic legend, 9,000 of Parthalon's people died of the plague and were buried in this place which was therefore called the *Taimh-leacht* or plague grave of Parthalon's people.

Tamlaght (also **Tamlat**), a plague grave; *see* Tallaght.

Tamnagh (also **Tamny**), *Tamhnach*, a green field.

Tandragee, a corruption of *Tóin-re-gaeith* (Tonregee), *backside* to the wind. *See* Tonlegee.

Tara, *Teamhair* (Tawer), F.M., a residence on an elevated spot commanding an extensive view. There are many places of this name in Ireland besides the celebrated Tara in Meath.

Tarmon, *see* Termon.

Tat (also **Tate**, **Tath**), a measure of land.

Tattygare, short *tate* or land measure.

Taughboyne, in Donegal: *Tech-Baeithin* (Taghbweeheen), O'C. Cal., the house of St *Baeithin;* he was a companion of St Columkille and governed the monastery of Iona after that saint's death. Died in AD 600.

Tavanagh (also **Tavnagh**), *Tamhnach*, a green field.

Tawlaght, a plague monument. *See* Tallaght.

Tawnagh (also **Tawny**), *Tamhnach*, a green field.

Tawnaghmore, great field.

Tecolm, in Laois: *Tigh-Choluim* (Teecolum). St Columkille's house.

Teebane, *Tigh-bán* (Teebaun), white house.

Teemore, greet house (*tigh*).

Teev (also **Teeve**), *Taebh*, the side, a hill side.

Teltown, on the Blackwater in Meath. Lewy of the Long Hand, one of the Tuatha De Danann kings, established a fair or gathering of the people to be held here yearly on the first of August in which games, pastimes and marriages were celebrated; and in honour of his foster mother *Taillte* (Telta), he called the place *Tailltenn* (Teltenn), now modernised to Teltown.

Temple, *Teampull*, a church.

Templeachally, in Tipperary: the church of the *cala* or marshy meadow.

Templebredon, in Tipperary: O'Bredon's church.

Templebreedy, St Brigid's church.

Templecarn, in Donegal: the church of the *carn* or monument

Temple-etney, in Tipperary: St Eithne's church.

Templemichael, the church of the Archangel Michael.

Templemolaga, in Cork: the church of St *Molaga*, a native of Fermoy, who died on the 20th January, some short time before the year 664.

Templemore, great church; a cathedral.

Templemoyle, bald or dilapidated church (*mael*).

Templenacarriaga, the church of the rock.

Templenoe (also **Templenew**), *Tampull-nua*, new church.

Templepatrick, St Patrick's church.

Templeport, the church of the *port* or bank.

Templeshanbo, in Wexford. Ancient pagan name *Seanboth-Sine* (Shanboh-Sheena), *Sin's* or Sheen's old tent or hut. In Christian times, after a church had been erected there, the present name was formed by the addition of the word *Temple* to *Seanboth*: Templeshanbo, the church of *Seanboth*.

Templetogher, in Galway: the church of the causeway (*tóchar*), from a celebrated old *togher* across a bog.

Templetuohy, in Tipperary: the church of the *tuath* or territory, because it was the principal church of the district.

Tempo, in Fermanagh: shortened from the full Irish name *an t-Iompodh-deisiol* (an Timpo deshill), the turning from left to right. *Iompodh* (impo) means turning, *deisiol*, right-handed, and the article *an* prefixed takes a *t* in this case, which became incorporated in the word. The place received its name, no doubt, from the ancient custom of turning sunways in worship.

Terenure, *Tir-an-iubhair*, the land of the yew.

Termon, *Tearmann*, church land.

Termonfeckin, St *Fechin's* church land.

Terryglass, in Tipperary: called in Irish authorities *Tir-da-ghlas* (Tir-a-glas), which Adamnan in his Life of St Columba translates *Ager-duorum-rivorum*, the land of the two streams.

Thurles, in Tipperary: *Durlios* (Durlas), strong *lis* or fort. In the annals it is commonly called Durlas-O'Fogarty, from the O'Fogartys, the ancient proprietors of the surrounding district. *See* Eliogarty.

Tiaquin, barony of, in Galway: shortened from *Tigh-Dachonna* (Tee-aconna), F.M., St Dachonna's house.

Tibohine, in Roscommon: *Teach-Baeithin* (O'C. Cal.), St *Baeithin's* house. The name is the same as Taughboyne, but this is a different *Baeithin;* he was of the race of *Enda*, son of Niall of the Nine Hostages, and was one of the ecclesiastics to whom the apostolic letter was written in the year 640 on the subject of the time for celebrating Easter.

Tieve, *Taebh* (teeve), a side, a hill-side.

Tievebrack, speckled hill-side.

Tiglin, in Wicklow: the house of the glen.

Tiknock (also **Ticknock**, **Ticknick**), *Tigh-cnuic* (Ticknick), the house of the hill.

Timahoe, in Laois: *Teach-Mochua* (Tee-Mohua), O'C. Cal., the house of St *Mochua*, the original founder and patron who flourished in the sixth century.

Timogue, in Laois: St Mogue's house.

Timoleague, in Cork: *Teach-Molaga*, F.M., *Molaga's* house, from St Molaga of Templemolaga.

Timolin, in Kildare: *Tigh-Moling* (Tee-Moling), St Moling's house, from a church erected there by St Moling of St Mullins.

Tinamuck, *Tigh-na-muc*, the house of the pigs.

Tincurragh (also **Tincurry**), *Tigh-an-churraigh* (Tincurry), the house of the *currach* or marsh.

Tinnahinch (also **Tinnehinch**), *Tigh-na-hinnse* (Tee-na-hin-sha), the house of the island or river meadow.

Tinnakill (also **Tinnakilly**), the house of the church or wood.

Tinnascart (also **Tinnascarty**), the house of the cluster or thicket (*scairt*).

Tinnick (also **Tinnock**, **Tinock**), *see* Tiknock.

Tipper, a form of *Tobar*, a well.

Tipperary, *Tiobraid-Arann* (Tibrad-Auran), F.M., the well of *Ara*, the ancient territory in which it was situated. The well that gave this name to the town and thence to the county was situated in the Main Street but it is now closed up.

Tipperkevin, in Kildare: St Kevin's well.

Tipperstown, in Dublin and Kildare: a half translation from *Baile-an-tobair* (Ballintubber), the town of the well.

Tiranascragh, in Galway: *Tir-an-eascrach*, the land of the *esker* or sand hill.

Tirawly, barony of, in Mayo: *Tir-Amhalgaidh* (Awly), the land or district of *Amhalgaidh*, king of Connaught, brother of the monarch *Dathi*, and son of Ohy Moyvane, king of Ireland from AD 358 to 365.

Tirconnell, the ancient name of Donegal, *Tir-Conaill*, the land or district of Conall Gulban, son of Niall of the Nine Hostages.

Tiveragh, barony of, in Sligo, *Tir-Fhiachrach* (Tir-eeragh), F.M., the district of *Fiachra*, son of *Dathi*, and grandson of Ohy Moyvane. *See* Tirawly.

Tirerrill, barony of, in Sligo, *Tir-Oiliolla* (ollila), Hy F., the district of Olioll, son of Ohy Moyvane (*see* Tirawly). *L* changed to *r*: *see* page 9.

Tirkeeran, barony of, in Derry: *Tir-Chaerthainn* (Tir-keerin), the district of Kieran, the great grandson of *Colla Uais*, brother of *Colla Meann*. *See* Cremorne.

Tisaran, in Offaly: from an old church which is called in the Calendars *Teach-Sarain* (Tasaran), the house of St Saran, the founder, who was of the race of the *Dealbhna*. *See* Delvin.

Tisaxon, the house of the Saxons or Englishmen.

Tiscoffin, in Kilkenny: *see* pages 9-10.

Tober, *Tobar*, a well.

Toberaheena, the well of Friday (*Aoine*, pron. eena); from the custom of visiting the well and performing devotions on Friday.

Toberbilly, the well of the ancient tree (*bile*).

Tobercurry, in Sligo: written by Mac Firbis, *Tober-an-Choire*, the well of the caldron or pit.

Tobermore, great well.

Toberreendoney, in various counties: *Tobar-righ-an-domhnaigh* (Toberreendowny), the well of the king of Sunday (i.e. of God); these wells were so called because they were visited on a Sunday.

Togher, *Tóchar*, a causeway.

Tomdeely, in Limerick: the tumulus (*tuaim*) of the river Deel.

Tomfinlough, in Clare: *Tuaim-Fionnlocha*, F.M., the tumulus of the bright lake (*fionn*, bright, clear); from an old church by a lake near Sixmilebridge.

Tomgraney, in Clare: *Tuaim-greine* (Toomgraney), F.M., the tumulus of the lady *Grian*, about whom there are many traditions.

Tomies mountain, over the lower lake of Killarney, *Tumaidhe* (Toomy), tumuli or monumental mounds; from two sepulchral heaps on the top of the mountain.

Tomregan, in Cavan: *Tuaim-Dhrecon* (toom-reckon: *D* aspirated – *see* page 7), F.M., Drecon's burial mound.

Tonagh, *Tamhnach* (Townagh), a field.

Tonbane (also **Tonbaun**), white *tóin* or *backside*.

Tonduff, black *backside* (*tóin*).

Tonlegee, *Tóin-le-gaeith*, backside to the wind.

Tonnagh, a mound or rampart.

Tonregee, *see* Tandragee and Tonlegee.

Tonroe, red backside.

Tooman, *Tuaman*, a small tumulus.

Toome (also **Toom**), *Tuaim* (Toom), a tumulus or burial mound.

Toomore (also **Toomour**), *Tuaim-dha-bhodhar* (Toom-a-wour), F.M., the tumulus of the two deaf persons.

Toomyvara, in Tipperary, exactly represents the sound of the Irish *Tuaim-ui-Mheadhra*, the tumulus or tomb of O'Mara.

Toor, *Tuar*, a bleach green or drying place.

Toorard, high bleach green.

Tooreen, little bleach green.

Toormore, great bleach green.

Toortane (also **Toortaun**), *Tortan*, a small hillock.

Tor, a tower, a tall tower-like rock.

Torc mountain at Killarney, the mountain of the *torcs* or boars.

Tormore, great tower or tower-like rock.

Tory island off the coast of Donegal, *Torach* (Wars of GG), towery, i.e. abounding in *tors* or tower-like rocks.

Touaghty, in Mayo: *Tuath-Aitheachta* (*Thoo-ahaghta*), Hy F., the *tuath* or district of the *attacotti* or plebeians, i.e. the races vanquished and enslaved by the Milesians.

Tourin, little bleach green; *see* Tooreen.

Tralee, *Traigh-Li* (Tralee), F.M., the strand of the Lee, a little river which runs into the sea at the town but which is now covered over.

Tramore, *Traigh-mor*, great strand.

Trean (also **Trien**), *Trian*, a third part.

Treanbaun, white third.

Treanboy, yellow third.

Treanlaur, middle third (*lár*, middle).

Treanmanagh, middle third (*meadhonach*).

Trevet, in Meath: *Trefoit* (Trefote), F.M., three *fods* or sods, so named, according to the *Leabhar-na-huidhre*, because when Art, the son of Conn of the Hundred Battles was buried there, three sods were dug over his grave in honour of the Trinity.

Trillick, *Tri-liag*, three *liags* or pillar stones.

Trim, in Meath; full name *Ath-truim* (Ah-trim), the ford of the elder bushes.

Tromaun, a place producing elder bushes (*trom*).

Trough, barony of, in Monaghan, *Triucha* (Truha), a cantred or district.

Trumman (also **Trummery**), *see* Tromaun.

Tuam, in Galway: *Tuaim-da-ghualann* (Tuam-a-woolan), the tumulus of the two shoulders, from the shape of the old sepulchral mound that gave name to the place.

Tubber, Galway *tobar* refers to a well or spring, sometimes a 'holy well'.

Tubbrid, *see* Tober.

Tulla (also **Tullach**), *Tulach*, a little hill.

Tullaghan, a little *tulach* or hill.

Tullaghmelan, in Tipperary: Moylan's hill.

Tullahogue, in Tyrone: *Tulach-óg*, F.M., the hill of the youths.

Tullahaught, in Kilkenny: *Tulach-ocht*, the hill of the eight (persons).

Tullamore, great hill.

Tullig, another form of *Tulach*, a hill.

Tullow, *Tulach*, a little hill.

Tullowphelim, a parish containing the town of Tullow in Carlow; contracted from Tullow-offelimy, the *tulach* or hill of the territory of the Hy Felimy, a tribe descended and named from Felimy, son of Enna Kinsella, king of Leinster in the fourth century.

Tully, *see* Tulla.

Tullyallen, *Tulaigh-áluinn* (Tullyaulin), beautiful hill.

Tullyard, high hill.

Tullybane (also **Tullybaun**), *Tulaigh-bán*, white hill.

Tullybeg, little *tulach* or hill.

Tullycorbet, the hill of the chariot (*carbad*).

Tullyglass, green hill.

Tullyhaw, barony of, in Cavan: so called from the Magaurans, its ancient proprietors, whose tribe name was *Tealach-Echach* (Tulla-eha: O'Dugan), the family of *Eochy* or Ohy.

Tullylease, in Cork: *Tulach-lias* (Tullaleese), the hill of the huts.

Tullymongan, at Cavan: *Tulach-Mongain*, F.M., Mongan's hill.

Tullymore, *see* Tullamore.

Tullynacross, the hill of the cross.

Tullynagardy, near Newtownards: *Tulaigh-na-gceard cha*, hill of the forges.

Tullynaskeagh, the hill of the white thorns.

Tullynure, *Tulach-an-uibhair*, the hill of the yew.

Tullyroe, red hill.

Tullyrusk, in Antrim: the hill on which the old church stands was surrounded by marshy ground, hence the name, which Colgan writes *Tulach-ruisc*, the hill of the morass. *See* Rusk.

Tullytrasna, cross or transverse hill.

Tumna, in Roscommon: *Tuaim-mna*, F.M., the tomb of the woman (*bean*, gen. *mna*).

Tuosist, in Kerry: *Tuath-O'Siosta* (O'Sheesta), O'Siosta's territory.

Ture, the yew. The word *iubhar* (yure) has incorporated the *t* of the article, like Tempo.

Turlough, a lake that dries up in summer.

Twelve Pins, a remarkable group of mountains in Connemara; should have been called the Twelve *Bens*, ie, peaks. Sometimes called 'The Twelve Pins of Bunnabola', in which the word *beann* occurs twice; for Bunnabola is *Beanna-Beola* (Banna-Bola), the peaks of *Beola*, an old Firbolg chief who is still remembered in tradition. *See* Mourne.

Tyfarnham, in Westmeath: *Farannan's* house (*tigh*); the same person that gave name to Multyfarnham.

Tyrella, in Down: *Tech-Riaghla* (Tee-Reela), O'C. Cal., the house of St *Riaghal* (Reeal) or Regulus.

Tyrone, in Tipperary: *Tigh-Eóin*, John's house.

Tyrone The descendants of *Eoghan* (Owen), son of Niall of the Nine Hostages, possessed the territory extending over the counties of Tyrone and Derry and the two baronies of Raphoe and Inishowen in Donegal; all this district was anciently called *Tir-Eoghain* (Tir-Owen: Wars of GG), Owen's territory, which is now written Tyrone, and restricted to one county. *See* Inishowen.

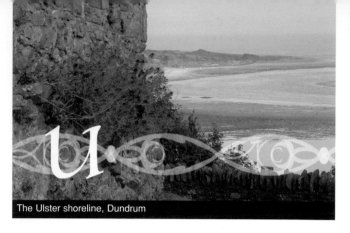
The Ulster shoreline, Dundrum

Ulster, ancient Irish form *Uladh* (ulla), which with *ster* added (*see* Leinster), was pronounced *Ulla-ster*, and contracted to Ulster.

Ummera (also **Ummery, Umry**), *Iomaire* (Ummera), a ridge.

Ummeracan (also **Umrycam**), *Iomaire-cam*, crooked ridge.

Ummerafree, the ridge of the heath (*fraech*).

Unshinagh (also **Inshinagh**), *Uinseannach*, a place producing ash trees (*uinnse* and *fuinnse*).

Uragh, *Iubhrach* (yuragh), yew land.

Urbal, a tail; from shape or position.

Urbalreagh, in Antrim, Donegal and Tyrone: grey tail.

Urbalshinny, in Donegal: the fox's tail (*sionnach*), from some peculiarity of shape, or perhaps from having been a resort of foxes.

Urcher, *Urchur*, a cast or throw. *See* Ardnurcher.

Uregare, in Limerick: *Iubhar-ghearr* (yure-yar), short yew tree.

Urney (also **Urny**), *Urnaidhe* (Urny), an oratory. *See* Nurney.

Urlar (also **Urlaur**), a floor, a level place.

Portmagee with Valentia Island in the distance.

Valentia Island, in Kerry: so called by the Spaniards. Ancient and present Irish name *Dairbhre* (Darrery), a place producing oaks. *See* Kildorrery.

Vartry river, in Wicklow: a corruption of the old tribe name *Fir-tire* (Firteera), the men of the territory (*tir*).

Ventry, in Kerry: got its name from a beautiful white strand called in Irish *Fionn-traigh* (Fintra), white strand.

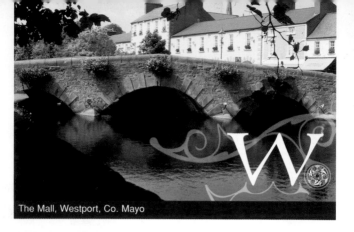
The Mall, Westport, Co. Mayo

Wateresk, upper channel (*eisc*). *See* Kilwatermoy.

Waterford, a Danish name; old form Vadrefiord, the latter part of which is the northern word *fiord*, a sea inlet. Old Irish name *Port-Lairge* or Portlargy. *See* Strangford and Carlingford.

Watergrasshill, in Cork: a translation of the Irish name Cnocán-na-biolraighe (Knockaun-na-billery), the little hill of the watercresses.

Westport, Mayo: in former times a centre for cattle trading, this west of Ireland port was called Cathair na Mart 'city of the beeves', or beef cattle.

Wexford, a Danish name; old form Weisford, which is said to mean west *fiord* or bay; old Irish name, *Carman*.

Wicklow, a Danish name; old forms of the name Wkyynglo, Wygyngelo, Wykinlo. Old Irish name Kilmantan, the church of St Mantan, one of St Patrick's disciples. This saint, according to the Annals of Clonmacnoise and other authorities, had his front teeth knocked out by a blow of a stone, from one of the barbarians who opposed St Patrick's landing in Wicklow; hence he was called *Mantan*, or the toothless.

Windgap (also **Windygap**), a translation of *Bearna-na-gaeithe* (Barnanageehy), the gap of the wind.

Witter, in Down: *Uachdar*, upper. *See* Wateresk and Eighter.

Wood of O, near Tullamore in Offaly: the Irish name is *Eóchaill*, yew-wood, the same as Youghal: modern name an attempted translation: Wood of O, i.e. the wood of the *eó* or yew.